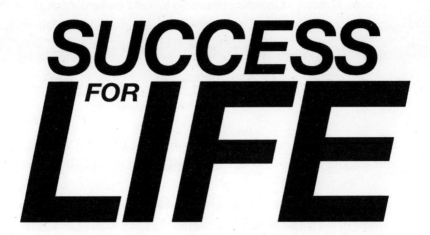

SUCCESS *FOR* LIFE

The Secret to Achieving Your True Potential

PAUL McKENNA DPhil

WELBECK

Published in 2024 by Welbeck
An imprint of Welbeck Non-Fiction Limited
Part of the Welbeck Publishing Group
Offices in: London – Carmelite House, 50 Victoria Embankment, EC4Y 0DZ
& Sydney – 205 Commonwealth Street, Surry Hills 2010
www.welbeckpublishing.com

A CIP catalogue record for this book is available from the British Library.

ISBN 978-1-80279-788-6

Illustrations by Ben Hasler, NB Illustration
Typeset by seagulls.net
Printed in Great Britain by CPI Books, Chatham, Kent

10 9 8 7 6 5 4 3 2 1

This book and audio programmes are intended for educational change. If you suspect you are suffering from a psychiatric disorder, contact your physician.

Important Note

You have bought this book for a reason, because you want to achieve more of your true potential every day and have a more amazing life. This guide contains everything I would do if I were working with you one-to-one. It will help you to access your ultimate state of being and live from it, which determines your success in life.

How to use this system

This book and the accompanying trance form two halves of a state-of-the-art system for success, allowing you to harness seven key super states of mind that will change your life for the better. Together, we will create an 'ultimate state' of being and help you to live from it in your daily life. Whether you start to achieve instant success or if the positive changes happen at a more gradual pace, every time you use your ultimate state you will be creating and reinforcing your success.

The first half of the system is contained in these pages, and it is important that you practise all the techniques until they become engrained in your being. If you have any trouble at all, there is a free audio version of each technique where I guide you through it step-by-step.

The second half of this system is a very special trance that I have created for you to accompany the book, containing a sophisticated but powerful matrix of hypnotic suggestions.

The trance works on two levels:

- It talks directly to your *left brain*, which is the seat of your logical, linear, and sequential thinking.

- It talks directly to your *right brain*, which is more focused on imagery, abstraction, and emotion.

All you really need to know is that throughout the trance I will be speaking to your *whole brain* at once. This amplifies the impact of the trance, speeding up your learning and making changing your life easier than ever.

There are only three steps to success:

1. Read the whole book at least once.

2. Do each technique at least twice.

3. Listen to the trance as often as you can.

As you follow each of these steps, you will start to notice that you see more opportunities, feel more confident and motivated, and begin to burst with optimism.

Life will seem less of a relentless struggle and become more and more amazing as your inner resources help you find surprising solutions to even your most challenging problems. You will begin to embrace your new world – a world filled with possibility where you are constantly a winner!

When you're ready to be guided through the techniques and listen to the trance, go to: www.paulmckenna.com/downloads and use the password:

success123

Contents

Introduction

If you were given a magic pill that suddenly gave you access to your true potential, would you take it? There was a hugely popular film called 'Limitless' released in 2011 where a man took such a drug to harness his brainpower and it changed everything for him. While I'm not aware if any such pill exists, there is another way to become the ultimate version of you using the extraordinary power of your mind and that is:

WHEN YOU ACCESS SEVEN KEY SUPER STATES AND STACK THEM ALL TOGETHER, YOU CREATE THE ULTIMATE STATE OF BEING AND THIS IS THE KEY TO UNLOCKING SUCCESS FOR LIFE.

The reason why this works is everything you achieve in life comes from your behaviours, and all your behaviours are driven by your emotional and physical state. For example, when a CEO handles a successful negotiation, an athlete wins at the Olympics or an artist performs brilliantly, it's because they are in their ultimate state of mind and body. I've found through my decades of working with super achievers that there are seven key super states that you can think of as psychological keys that will unlock your 'A-game'. They are: **self-belief, clarity, determination, connection, creativity, 'energy & health' and happiness.** When you stack one on top of another, it's like having an inner super power. As when they are combined, they create what athletes and business super achievers call 'being in the zone' while musicians and those in creative industries call it 'being in the groove or flow'. This is the ultimate state of being – and you will be able to access yours by the end of this book. It changes everything, even down to your posture, feelings and the quality of the thoughts you have. It will make you a winner in life. Each of the seven chapters of this book will add one super state to your own ultimate state of being.

I've designed this method after working with some of the most elite minds in the world. I have learned and codified their strategies and frame of mind. As I take you through each section of this book you will evoke and then experience how fantastic each super state feels. At the end of each chapter, I will then ask you to envision your new, dazzling future from that empowered place. Chapter by chapter, as we stack the seven super states together, like building blocks, your future will become better and brighter. I will also teach you a powerful process called 'anchoring' that means by the end of this book, tapping into your ultimate state of being will literally be at your fingertips. You can think of anchoring as being like a light switch that you can turn on and off. So, whenever you press your thumb and middle finger together you can call upon it at will. The trance that accompanies this guide will then reinforce this process and take it deep into your unconscious mind to exponentially increase its benefits. So even if you're completely sceptical, don't be too surprised if your future becomes one beyond your wildest dreams right now. As together, we are going to unleash the ultimate version of you. You may have stumbled upon this state of being in the past, or experienced a few moments of it, without recognising what it was. By the time you finish this book you will not only know what it is, but you will be living it.

In the few hours it will take you to read this guide and do the exercises you will become an even better version of yourself. Your ultimate state of being will also grow over time and impact the future in every area of your life. Whether you are already ultra-successful or you feel you want more out of life, things are about to get better than you ever dreamed previously. You will move beyond your perceived limits, embrace your inner genius, harness your creativity, get highly motivated, determined and resilient. You will be primed to act on opportunities that come your way and embrace success. You will also rediscover your inner happy place. If at any time you wonder how well it's working, that's just your old limitations adjusting to the new boundaries of your ultimate self.

This book is unlike any of my previous 'I Can Make You...' series, which have trained millions of people to become thin, rich, confident and even sleep. This is a holistic guide where I will support you to unlock your own ultimate state of being. Think of it as a set of personal coaching sessions. Coaching is when you elicit from *within* someone their own resources and help direct and manage them. So, as I coach you, you will be in control as you work through this powerful process.

There can only be two things that have stopped you from realising your true potential up to this point. The first is that you can't imagine just how amazing your life really can be. Or secondly, perhaps you have been unconsciously self-sabotaging or holding yourself back as there's a part of you that somehow doesn't believe that you deserve success or is frightened of what it would be like. But remember, as you do the techniques and listen to the audio downloads – particularly the hypnotic trance – you will undergo an exciting transformation. By the time you finish this book you will have all the tools you need to become the person you were meant to be. Together we will design and create a new life picture, based around your core values to give you an even greater sense of meaning and purpose.

A common misconception I want to address right from the outset, is that being the best version of yourself means you've got to be some kind of superhuman workaholic who sacrifices parts of their life in some way. That simply isn't the case. Mahatma Gandhi once said: "There is more to life than simply increasing its speed". So, while this method might involve trying some new things, it *isn't* about working harder. It's about working *smarter.*

These pages also take you into my world. I'm going to pass on what I've learned in my three decades as a hypnotherapist and success coach. I'm also going to share a series of anecdotes I've gleaned from the conversations I've been fortunate to have through my work as an interviewer, radio DJ and podcaster with super achievers including those from the Arts, Science, Business and Sport to inspire you.

As you start your transformation there's just one more thing I want to stress. There is only one way you won't get the results you want and that is to not finish this book. If you keep going, every chapter will build on the one before. You need *all* of the super states in order to create your ultimate state of being. So don't skip ahead, just follow the process to the end. It's literally that simple. Just a few hours of your life will make all the difference. My intention is that everyone who reads this book, does the techniques and listens to the trance will realise: "Life is more amazing than I ever thought possible before".

The role of Neuro Linguistic Programming in this book

When you change on the inside then everything on the outside changes. It's as simple as that. Unfortunately, the majority of people are trying to get their external world to conform to what they want. So, they spend all their time and energy attempting to manipulate it. To a greater or lesser extent, they are able to achieve that – but it's very hard work. It's much more effective to transform how you *think* and *feel* in order to get yourself into an awesome state of mind and body. We create an internal world with our imagination, memories and our inner voice, which can have a massive impact on how we perceive our external world. So, this process will change your perceptions and your focus and that, in turn, will change your life.

Throughout this process we will use a series of techniques from the world of Neuro Linguistic Programming or NLP. 'Neuro' stands for neurological, 'Linguistic' represents a way of communicating and 'Programming' relates to the fact that just as a computer has programs in order to do things, human beings do too. So, everything you do from boiling an egg to making a million pounds comes down to your Neuro Linguistic Programming. By using specific NLP techniques, we can change the programs that we are running internally. Many of the programs we have support us and they are functional and positive, such as the action of opening a door or shaking hands. But many people also run negative programs, which include things like emotional eating, or smoking, as coping mechanisms for stress.

In NLP we are not interested in *'why?'* in the way old-fashioned analysis tried to approach change – for example, *why* are you over-eating, *why* are you depressed? Instead, we are interested in *'how?'* for instance; *how* do you moti-vate or depress yourself? *How* do you get creative? *How* do you concentrate? We also know that everything that is going on inside you at any one moment creates how you feel, think and behave. NLP is a technology for under-standing it and changing it.

As well as using NLP techniques to change unwanted behaviours we can also use it to further enhance the posi-tive programs that we already have. Many of the super achievers I have worked with are already the best at what they do in the world, but they want to be *even better*. I used NLP with them to get them into a peak state of performance so that whenever they step out to perform on stage at an arena, or compete at the Olympics, or negotiate in the arena of global business, they are primed for success. By using a sequence of pictures, sounds and physiology in a particular algorithm or sequence, I coached them to create their own ultimate state of being. And that's what I'm going to do with you. Every major sports person and many global CEOs have success coaches or therapists – someone like me working with them. Now you do too!

Creating your anchor

I've mentioned that during this process I'm going to show you how to capture and have literally at your fingertips your new ultimate state of being. Anchoring is one of the simplest, yet most effective NLP techniques to do this. So, I'm going to ask you at times when you are in the peak of harnessing each of the seven super states to anchor it by getting you to squeeze your thumb and middle finger together. Anchoring works by linking physical touch to an empowering feeling or behaviour you want to be able to call upon at will. It is a type of associational link, which is one of the brain's shortcuts.

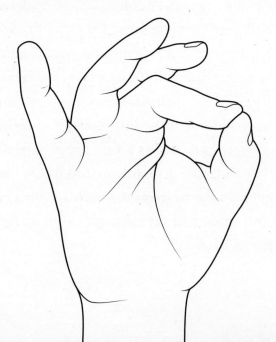

The most famous associational link research in history is Ivan Pavlov's dogs. During the 1890s, he noticed dogs would salivate whenever food was being brought to them. So, Pavlov started to ring a bell at feeding time – creating an associational loop between the bell and food. He'd ring the bell and feed the dogs and he repeated that process again and again. Eventually when he only rang the bell the dogs' mouths would salivate. In the same way, we can use the extraordinary power of association to boost good feelings, increase confidence and performance. So, think of an anchor as one element of an experience that can bring back a whole experience. For example, a song on the radio can remind you of an old romance or a holiday, bringing back in your mind's eye that whole experience. If I'm driving to an airport, even if I'm only dropping someone off, I still get a tingle of excitement as I associate it with travel, which I love. Through the repetition of squeezing together our middle finger and thumb we can really cement that association. So, there's no logical reason for the thumb and middle finger squeeze to be linked to good feelings but nonetheless repetition makes a link happen. In the same way, this is how people get hardwired to habits like smoking, as when a smoker is stressed, they reach for a cigarette. Or if you feel upset and eat cake, after a while emotional eating becomes a habit.

The actor Stephen Fry, who has a massive passion for the arts, used a fabulous associational link alongside my weight loss system to get thinner. He followed my method but also purchased the 100 audio books that he most wanted to listen to and only played them while he was on the treadmill. So rather than feeling bored, his unconscious mind began to associate the treadmill with the excitement of listening to Shakespeare or the latest best seller. I thought what a fantastic way to create a positive associational link!

In the same way, by repeatedly anchoring the seven super states, when you finish this book, you will be able to call upon them at will and they will become a part of who you are. This process will combine them all together to make one ultimate state of being where everything goes stratospheric. So, by the time you turn the final page and listen to the trance you will be able to press your thumb and middle finger together to call upon your ultimate state of being on demand! It works because you are hard-wiring yourself to experience those fabulous feelings in an 'empowering loop'. So now let's get started. It's time to build your best life.

Chapter One

Self-Belief

To start with, we are going to clear any blocks to success in your unconscious mind by doing a simple technique to ensure you are fully open to the amazing change that's going to happen. Then, we're going to add the state of self-belief as the first building block of your ultimate state of being.

As I mentioned previously, there are two things in life that stop people from achieving. One is self-sabotage. The other is not thinking *big* enough. It's only when you start running possibilities within the realm of what you *think* you deserve, *think* you can handle, or *think* is possible that you can empower yourself. So, it's time to begin to take the limiters off and stretch your perceived boundaries, which installing **self-belief** will do for you. Self-belief is a state where you have confidence in your own abilities and judgement. Once you have harnessed it, you'll discover that you can do way more than you previously imagined.

Seeing beyond
your boundaries

So, let's firstly clear any obstacles that stand in your way. This is because if you think you *can't* do something you *won't*. These obstacles can take the form of internal conflict or self-sabotage. The person most likely to sabotage you from getting the life you want is *you*. So, now, we're going to change that. You see, more often than not, limiting thoughts are constructs of our own mind. What's behind it is almost always an unconscious pattern of protection.

One of my clients experienced an extreme example of this. As a child he told his mother: "When I grow up, I want to be successful". She replied: "Oh you don't want to do that, son, successful people have heart attacks". That throwaway remark became implanted in his unconscious mind like a hypnotic suggestion, said by an authority figure at an impressionable age. When he got older, every time he was on the brink of success, he'd botch things up. The reason this happened is the unconscious mind is not logical, it is *purposeful*. Its intent is always positive, and in this case, its purpose was survival! So even though it is completely illogical to think that all successful people have heart attacks, his unconscious mind thought: "Hang on a minute, we're starting to get successful. I'd better stop this or I'm going to die!". It thought it was saving him!

While that's an extreme case, many people feel torn in their lives. It's like driving down the street but continually slamming on the brakes. It makes for a bumpy ride through life. As you overcome self-sabotage, you will be able to gently ease between the accelerator and the brake and have a smoother ride through each day.

Significant experiences that take place in the first few years of our life can shape our personality, character and self-belief. Aristotle is often quoted as saying: "Give me a child until he is seven and I'll show you the man". It's known as childhood conditioning. The conditioning we experience from our youth and beyond floats around in our unconscious mind – which is a bit like a sea of thoughts. So, if, for example, someone gets hurt in a relationship, they can then go on to sabotage later relationships. I was fantastic at exactly that for years! As soon as things started to go well, I would mess it up. This was because deep down, I didn't want to feel out of control. So, there is a whole load of reasons why our unconscious might stop us fulfilling our potential but remember, more often than not, they are not logical ones. Recognising that is the first step to fixing it.

If you are reading these words but you are also experiencing some reservations, trepidation or conflict about embracing success for life right now, then don't worry! That's actually understandable, as you may have been conditioned to have ideas about success that just aren't true.

So now I will take you through a very simple exercise, which will help you resolve any internal conflict, self-sabotage or unnecessary hesitation you may be feeling about becoming truly successful in your own life. I recently used it to help a lady at one of my seminars who was locked in this cycle. She said: "I'd like my career to take off and to be happier, but I keep blowing it". She didn't know why she was doing it. The good news is, even if you don't have a clue about what is stopping you, we can still fix it. So, I did this simple process with her. I asked her to visualise the part of her that was self-sabotaging and put it into one hand. Then I asked her to visualise the other part of her that wanted to succeed and put it into the other hand. (It's not that there are two different people inside you – it's just a way of illus-trating aspects that are parts of yourself.) I then asked her to bring both parts together (so she literally brought both of her hands together to represent this). Boom! Quickly, her unconscious mind was able to find ways for both parts to co-exist and fulfil their positive intentions.

This technique is deceptively simple, but it 'speaks' to the unconscious and leads internal conflict to be resolved. I saw her six months later and not only had she rebooted her career, she was in a relationship, lost weight and looked and felt fantastic. I could give you hundreds and hundreds of examples of how this process, known as the Visual Squash, devised by NLP co-founder Dr Richard Bandler, has transformed people's lives. So, let's do it now.

OVERCOMING SELF-SABOTAGE

🔊 *Read through this technique before you do it.*
If you want me to guide you through it, download the
free audio at: paulmckenna.com/downloads

1　Put your hands out in front of you, palms facing up.

2　In your dominant hand, put the part of you that wants to succeed and fulfil your true potential.

3　Next, in the other hand, put the part that stops you or sabotages you.

POSITIVE INTENTION　　SABOTAGE

4　Now, bring your hands together and let the two parts sit together for a while so they can figure out, at the unconscious level, how they

POSITIVE INTENTION　　SABOTAGE

can both achieve their positive intentions for you without being in conflict with each other. Take all the time you need.

5 Eventually, it will feel like there's a click, or a feeling that it's possible that these two parts can work together.

6 Next, bring your hands towards your chest and integrate this new super part into you.

SUPER
PART

7 Now, start to imagine how your life will be so much better, free from self-sabotage and able to fulfil your true potential in all areas.

This exercise is a great one to come back to if at any point during the book, or after you've completed it, you notice yourself thinking that things are almost going too well or if you feel any internal conflict or hesitation.

This technique is used with the written permission of Dr Richard Bandler.

The power of a positive self-image

Now we've removed sabotage or hesitation it's time to begin to install your super state of self-belief. This, in turn, will create a new, positive self-image. When we refer to the 'self-image' it means a blueprint for who we think we are but more importantly for what we *believe* we can and can't do. If you are told at an impressionable age, by someone in authority that you're artistic, you are likely to become it. It becomes part of who you believe you are and therefore more likely to happen. Equally, experiences of emotional intensity – again, at an impressionable age – that leave you making a judgement about yourself can also affect your self-identity. So, if you win a competition and decide, 'I'm lucky', or win a race, and decide, 'I'm good at sport', that shapes you too. So having a positive self-image is critical to a successful life.

Actress and producer Priyanka Chopra Jonas is a model of excellence in her field and self-belief is a key ingredient of her success mindset. She told me: "The little failures are not going to define the collective whole of who I am."

She describes her other qualities as including: "Discipline, a sense of not being entitled. Working hard for everything that you achieve without expecting for it to happen. Creating opportunities. I think the one very important thing that I inherited from my dad was my sense of adventure. I don't get daunted when I have to move countries…continents and live out of a suitcase for years and meet new people. I see it as a sense of adventure. From my mum, she always said to have your own courage and conviction. So, whether it's the right decision or the wrong decision, it's your decision. And you have to stand by that. I'm the sum of my successes and not of my failures." She is someone who is harnessing her true potential and living in her ultimate state of being. That has manifested into her leading an extraordinary life that she loves.

Remember, if you have picked up some limiting beliefs about your self-identity, you need to think of them as being like a minor glitch in a computer program. The good news is that your brain can be re-programmed, just like a computer can. This NLP technique will get you to step into the life of someone who is an ultra-achiever. It needs to be someone who is living an optimal life you'd like to emulate. Through visualisation, you can empower yourself with their attributes. Perhaps it's someone like Priyanka, or a football genius like Lionel Messi. Maybe it's a super creative singer-songwriter like Ed Sheeran or a dazzlingly successful entrepreneur like Oprah Winfrey. It doesn't matter if you know them or not, they simply have to be a model of excellence. It doesn't even have to be someone famous, it could be your Aunty Gladys!

Because your nervous system doesn't know the difference between reality and a vividly imagined experience, when you step into your role model and experience life from their perspective, something really amazing happens. That simple process begins to program into *your* brain the optimised state they operate in. To amplify their positive state of mind and body, we'll imagine giving the good feelings they experience a colour and then spread that colour from the top of your head to the tips of your toes. Let's try it now.

STEP INTO YOUR ROLE MODEL

🔊 *Read through this technique before you do it.*
If you want me to guide you through it, download the
free audio at: paulmckenna.com/downloads

1. Think of someone who operates at their true potential, or close to it.

2. Now imagine them standing in front of you.

3. Next, imagine stepping into them and *see* the world through their eyes, *hear* their internal dialogue and *feel* how they feel.

4. Notice where they feel best in their body and as you feel that, experience it for yourself.

5. Next, give that good feeling a colour.

continued

6   Now imagine spreading that good feeling up to the top of your head and down to the tip of your toes.

7   Now double the brightness of the colour.

8   Now, while you are in this peak state of mind and body, squeeze your thumb and middle finger together and hold them together while you feel this good. Do it several times to create a strong associational link.

Open your mind to possibility

Now you've overcome self-sabotage and you've begun the process of stepping into the new you, it's time to expand your horizons. Many people habitually repeat the same behaviours through life as they have got a template and a selection of strategies they work from. Quite simply, they limit themselves without realising. To start the process of unshackling you from what's currently holding you back, I'd like to ask a simple question:

WHAT WOULD YOU DO IF YOU KNEW YOU COULDN'T FAIL?

When I was a radio DJ back in the '80s I was successful and I loved my job. But at the same time, I had a feeling that something was missing but I lacked the self-belief to throw in the towel and start something completely different. Through my radio work I met a hypnotist and when I saw first-hand the potential it had for helping people as a tool for positive change, it blew my mind. So, when I just couldn't shake off that feeling, I asked myself that question and I took the limiters off and let my mind dream up a

fantastic life for myself. I decided I'd love to be a hypnotist on television. I wanted to make self-improvement tapes
(there was no streaming back then!), travel the world and
work with amazing people including rock stars, movie
icons, athletes and CEOs. By really interrogating myself,
I was able to *dream big*. For the first time in my life, I worked
out what I truly wanted. Then I devised a strategy to make
it happen and I acted on it. I've made my dream a reality
and if I can do it, anyone can. That's why I've created this
book and audio programme.

Throughout history numerous trailblazers have dreamed
beyond their perceived limits and created something amazing or a legacy. A famous quote often attributed to Henry
Ford says: "If I had asked people to tell me what they
wanted they would have said a faster horse and buggy". Back
then, if he'd had a focus group on what people *wanted* they
would have chosen a better version of what people already
used to travel around in, as that was all that they knew. But
Henry Ford opened his mind and went on to create a true
innovation – he created the first motorcar and changed the
modern world. Other massive successes that were innovations of their time include CNN, which became the world's
first 24-hour news network. It was dubbed 'Chicken Noodle
Network' by critics in the early days as they believed it

wouldn't last. Others include *The X Factor* and even Post-it Notes and what's interesting about each of them is that they all failed focus groups because they were so totally creative, yet they became phenomenal successes.

Other innovative businesses faced massive criticism or were ridiculed, yet went on to change the face of their industries. In 2021 Jeff Bezos posted on X (formerly Twitter) the front page of a 1999 business and financial newspaper emblazoned with the headline "Amazon.Bomb". He wrote alongside it: "This was just one of the many stories telling us all the ways we were going to fail. Today Amazon is one of the world's most successful companies and has revolutionised two entirely different industries.

More recently, fragrance entrepreneur Jo Malone created fragrance paintbrushes so people could paint scent like artists onto their bodies. It was an innovation that changed the industry. She once told me: "I visualise my dreams and my aspirations and then I'll make them a reality". All of these different industries have one thing in common. They had an individual, or a group of people, who had a shared belief in what they were trying to do. Like Henry Ford, Jeff and Jo, I am going to be asking you to believe in yourself, dream big, harness your creative genius and use that new-found intelligence to manifest a life more wonderful than you'd thought possible before.

So, stop for a few moments and imagine the following. The more specific you are, the better. Many people find that it helps to write this down and return to it later so it can inspire them. It will also evolve over time.

DISCOVERING YOUR BEST SELF

 Grab a pen and answer the following questions.

How would your life be if you were achieving more of your true potential?

How would your mental and physical health be?

How would your relationships be?

continued

How would your career be?

How would your finances be?

How happy would you feel?

Visualising the new, empowered you has taken you a step closer to reality. Next, we are going to begin to consider what you are truly capable of in order to manifest a richer life filled with more joy, purpose, passion and fulfilment.

Creating your ultimate state of being

Now it's time to install self-belief as the first building block of your ultimate state of being by visualising the new you fulfilling your potential. You have already stepped into the mindset of a super achiever. Now we are going to use the same idea to step into the new you. Using this simple process I will ask you to imagine you are watching a cinema screen and on that screen you can see the new you who is performing at your peak. I'll ask you: How do you stand? How do you sit? How do you gesture? What does your voice sound like? Then I'm going to get you to float into that new you and see through your eyes, hear the internal dialogue and feel how it feels and by playing it through you can imagine even greater potential. You'll do this three times. This is because, sometimes when you say to someone "Imagine yourself at your true potential", it's hard to do that straightaway. But if you do it in stages, you can push much further than you initially envisaged.

EXPERIENCING YOUR
TRUE POTENTIAL

🔊 *Read through this technique before you do it.*
If you want me to guide you through it, download the
free audio at: paulmckenna.com/downloads

STAGE 1

1   Imagine a cinema screen in front of you.

2   Imagine watching a movie on the screen
    of a new you that is operating at your true
    potential, or close to it.

3   Notice your posture, the expression on your
    face, the light behind your eyes, the sound of
    your voice, the way you gesture, connect with
    others, everything that lets you know you are
    in an amazing state of mind and body.

4   Now, float over and into that new you on the screen.

5   *See* through the eyes of your true potential self, *hear* your internal dialogue and *feel* how good it feels to be in this amazing state of mind and body.

6   Notice the area where you feel best in your body.

continued

7   Next, give that good feeling a colour.

8   Now imagine spreading that good feeling up to the top of your head and down to the tip of your toes.

9   Now *double* the brightness of the colour.

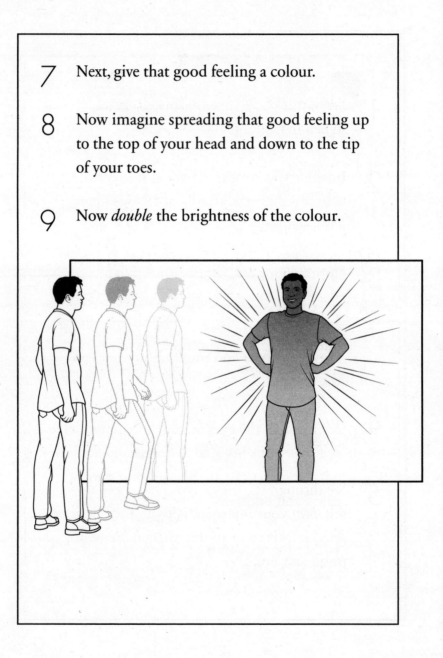

STAGE 2

1   From this place, imagine, once again, a cinema screen in front of you.

2   Imagine watching a movie on the screen of a new you that is operating at an even higher level, achieving even more.

3   Notice your posture, the expression on your face, the light behind your eyes, the sound of your voice, the way you gesture, connect with others, everything that lets you know you are in an amazing state of mind and body.

4   Now, float over and into that you on the screen.

5   *See* through the eyes of your true potential self, *hear* your internal dialogue and *feel* how good it feels to be in this amazing state of mind and body.

continued

6   Notice the area where you feel best in your body.

7   Next, give that good feeling a colour.

8   Now imagine spreading that good feeling up to the top of your head and down to the tip of your toes.

9   Now *double* the brightness of the colour.

STAGE 3

1   Now let's really enhance your state even more…

2   No matter how good you're feeling, once again, imagine a cinema screen in front of you.

3   Imagine watching a movie on the screen of a new you that is operating at an even higher level.

4   Notice your posture, the expression on your face, the light behind your eyes, the sound of your voice, the way you gesture, connect with others, everything that lets you know you are in an amazing state of mind and body.

5   Now, float over and into that you on the screen.

6   *See* through the eyes of your true potential self, *hear* your internal dialogue and *feel* how good it feels to be in this amazing state of mind and body.

7   Notice the area where you feel best in your body.

8   Next, give that good feeling a colour.

9   Now imagine spreading that good feeling up to the top of your head and down to the tip of your toes.

10 Now double the brightness of the colour.

11 Now, while you are in this peak state of mind and body, squeeze your thumb and middle finger together and hold them together while you feel this good. Pause, and take as long as you want, in order to fully experience and remember the amazing feelings that go with it. Do it several times to create a strong associational link.

You have now harnessed the first of your seven super states and you are a step closer to creating your ultimate state of being. You will already be feeling great. Take a moment to acknowledge those positive feelings. But remember, things are about to get even better. When you are ready, you can start the next chapter to discover and harness your super state of *clarity* and in doing so, gain key insights about yourself and what your life will be like when you are living in an optimal state of mind and body.

Chapter Two

Clarity

Now we are going to harness your second super state of *clarity* and add it to your ultimate state of being. When you get a laser-sharp focus about what you want in life, harness your inner genius and understand what truly matters, you are in that super state.

I very often speak to people who tell me that they're not sure what they want, or they're conflicted, unfulfilled, or something indefinable is missing. Getting clear about your future and why you want it is vital in order to give you the motivation to attain it. That is the focus of this chapter.

The four zones of genius

A fundamental thing you need to know when it comes to finding clarity in your life is that we all have an inner genius. Yet, if I was to ask most people: *'What are you truly brilliant at?'* the vast majority initially would struggle to answer. Gay Hendricks calls it 'The Upper Limit Problem'. It's effectively a glass ceiling to fulfilling your true potential that many people don't even realise they have. Gay explains: "Even if you are already amazingly successful, I can promise you that your own version of the Upper Limit Problem is still holding you back from achieving your true potential". So, let's change it and take charge of your inner genius!

One of my favourite examples of breaking an upper limit problem is the four-minute mile – something that experts said for years the human body was simply not capable of doing. Yet Sir Roger Bannister did it in 1954. As part of his training, he visualised the achievement. He mentally prepared himself for success. Interestingly, he didn't know how close he was to reaching it and his trainers didn't tell him either. If he'd known he might have inhibited himself – it's all about the power of belief. What's really interesting is that within 13 months of his historic race, a further six athletes also broke the four-minute mile. To date, more than 1,664 athletes have accomplished what was once thought to be the limits of human capability. New Zealand athlete Nick Willis has also matched his record every year for the past two decades in a row! So, what changed for so many people to break through that glass ceiling? It's clearly not that humanity in the space of just over a year became much more physically fit. It's because others gained self-belief that they too could achieve it, because someone else had proved it was possible. When I met Sir Roger, I asked him: "Is it true that you didn't know your running times beforehand?" And he said: "Yes, it is. I was hopeful I was going to do it but I was running good times in practice and when I did it, it was amazing." I then said: "I also find it amazing that so many other people went on to do it," and he replied: "Yes, it's incredible isn't it". He smashed an Upper Limit Problem paving the way for others to follow!

A story often told about the inventor Thomas Edison also illustrates the power of self-belief and harnessing your inner genius. Among his inventions Edison created the incandescent light bulb and the motion picture camera as well as improving the telephone. Yet in his lifetime he only spent a matter of months attending school. One day, the story goes, he took a letter home to his mum Nancy from his teacher. When he asked her what it contained she told him it said: "Your son is a genius" and that he was so clever that she needed to teach him herself. That's what she did. And Edison went on to become one of the world's greatest inventors. After his mother died, Edison reportedly found that letter among her personal papers. Instead of containing what she'd claimed, it apparently said he was 'addled' – a term used in those days for a lack of clarity of the mind – and he was expelled from school. The story goes that upon discovering the truth Edison made an entry in his own diary saying: "Thomas A Edison was a mentally deficient child whose mother turned him into the genius of the century". Because Edison's mother told him he was a genius she installed self-belief. He also wasn't limited by the beliefs of his former teacher so he harnessed his inner genius and went on to achieve the impossible.

Similarly to Edison, George Bernard Dantzig also spectacularly crashed through an Upper Limit Problem by not being limited by others which enabled him to harness his inner genius. He arrived late for a statistics class and found two problems written on the chalkboard. He assumed they were homework, so he jotted them down and worked on them over the weekend. What he didn't realise was they were actually 'unsolved' problems and he cracked one of them because he didn't know it wasn't possible. He became known as the Accidental Maths Genius!

Gay says the only way to conquer *your* upper limit problem and stretch beyond your perceived limits is to take a leap into what he calls The Four Zones Of Genius. It gets you thinking outside of the box about yourself. My friend, life coach and fellow author Michael Neill did a version of Gay's process on me years ago when I felt a bit stuck. He drew four squares and in the first one in the top right-hand corner he asked me to put something I was really bad at. In the bottom right square he asked me to put something I wasn't particularly good or bad at, in the bottom left-hand corner, I put something I was good at and in the top left I put something I was totally brilliant at. This takes you, in increments, into the sudden realisation that you are actually great at something. That, in turn, propels you towards your true potential by installing self-belief. I've done this process with people from all walks of life through the years, including super achievers. Everyone gets to recognise that they are really brilliant at something and often it's an attribute they had previously taken for granted. Once you discover yours, it will supercharge your confidence and help you to spiral upwards towards ever increasing success.

THE FOUR ZONES OF GENIUS

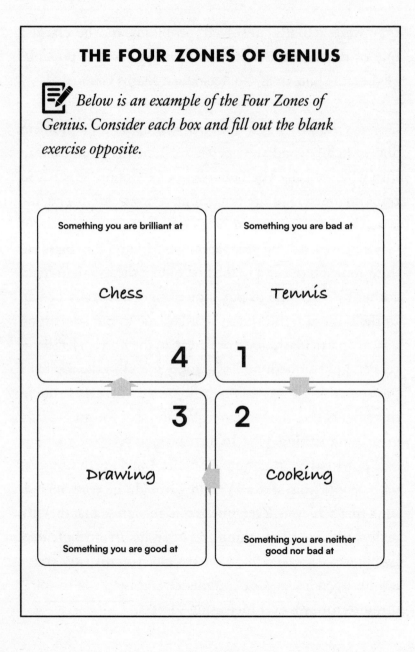

Below is an example of the Four Zones of Genius. Consider each box and fill out the blank exercise opposite.

Something you are brilliant at

Chess

4

Something you are bad at

Tennis

1

3

Drawing

Something you are good at

2

Cooking

Something you are neither good nor bad at

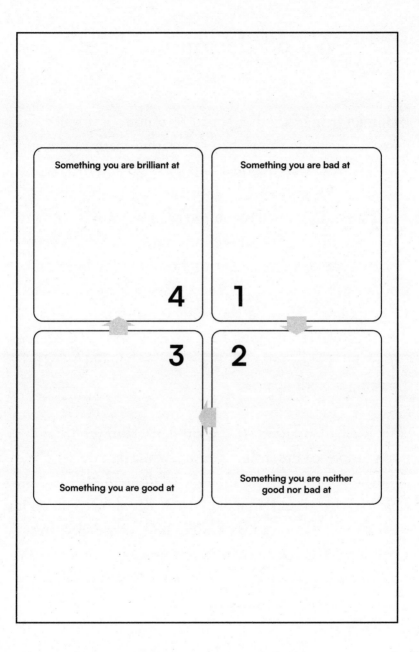

Something you are brilliant at

Something you are bad at

4

1

3

2

Something you are good at

Something you are neither
good nor bad at

We all design our lives

Human beings are thought to be unique as a species as we can imagine things before creating them in the real world. So, we can trial ideas in our mind and then act on what's going to work in reality. The chef Heston Blumenthal famously created bacon and egg ice cream in this way. He combined self-belief with his inner creative, entrepreneurial and culinary genius to dream outside boundaries of normality – and it became a massive hit with foodies! I asked him: "How do you come up with these fantastic creations?" He told me, "I ask myself: *'What will happen if...?'* It's a great question that everyone should ask when starting something new.

Sir Richard Branson used a similar technique when he revolutionised the airline industry. While on a dreary plane journey in the '70s he thought to himself: "If I had an airline what would it be like?" He believed he could do it better. So, he made a list of things he'd want on his dream passenger flight. It included giving everyone their own TV and a really good headset, better food, amazing staff, a bar in the plane and a pre-flight lounge you'd look forward to going to. By the time his flight landed he had designed in his mind the blueprint for Virgin Airlines. He believed in himself, harnessed his business genius, designed his dream in his mind and he changed aviation history.

Whether you are consciously aware of it or not, we are all designers in our own lives. When you drive a car, you create a journey and when you cook a meal you create an experience – and if you think it's going to be bad it often is! Even if what you are creating is your own unhappiness you have a say in the world you inhabit. So, consider this reframe. From the moment you wake up in the morning until the moment you go to sleep, acknowledge you can have a massive influence in designing your life. Then start to act on it. Only around 50 per cent of what we do each day is a habit which is highly necessary and functional (such as when you clean your teeth or tie your shoelaces). That leaves a lot of room for influence!

What truly matters to you

To help you visualise and design your best possible future you need to make a distinction between your goals and what truly matters to you (your values). Goals are important, but only when they are built on the bedrock of your deepest values. What's truly important to you is the core of who you believe you are. It is also a powerful driver for change and attaining success. When you live by what truly matters, you will experience a sense of fulfilment, purpose and happiness. Yet all too often, people confuse these two very different things. For example, often when I ask people what they want to achieve, they'll say: "I want to earn as much money as possible." But that is a goal, not a value. So, in order to find out what's really important in their life, I'll then ask them what the money will get for them, give them, or do for them. They might then reply: "It will give me a feeling of *security* and *achievement*." Both things represent what's truly important to them, so they are their values. Values are the things that enrich your life spiritually, as opposed to acquisitions. I recently saw a programme about one of the greatest investors and philanthropists of all time: Warren Buffett. He bought his first stocks and shares at 11 years old and is now worth an estimated $120.1 billion according to Forbes. He's promised to donate 99 per cent of his wealth and so far, he has given more than $51 billion. When he was asked what's the secret to his success he replied: "I can tell you in one word. Focus." He's using his extraordinary wealth to make a difference in the world so he's clear about his aims and living from his own values.

In order to help you define your own values which will be the bedrock of your future success, let me share my own experience. I used to be a relentless goal setter and I wasn't in touch with my values. This meant I continually put off being happy until I reached the next career objective, but once I got there, there was always another goal to attain. Everything from my happiness, gratitude, fulfilment and even security was put on hold as I was always chasing the next big thing... then the next... and then the next! When I changed my behaviour and became focused on what truly mattered to me, it was a eureka moment in my life. I realised *values* are what makes me truly successful and happy. My personal values are health, love, laughter, loyalty, gratitude, generosity and creativity. So, I consciously try to tick the box every day of the following questions: Do I feel healthy mentally and physically? Do I feel loved by my family and friends and do they know my love for them? Did I laugh out loud? Was I creative in some way? Did I experience gratitude? Was I kind, loyal or helpful? When I am ticking my value boxes, I feel I'm truly winning.

I've met far too many people (including many multi-millionaires!) who are unhappy because they are only ever living a goal-based life. I've also met some very happy millionaires and that's because they are living by their values. When I wrote my book *I Can Make You Rich*, I spoke to the late Sir David Barclay, and he said to me: "You are going to meet a whole load of people while you are working on this book who are wealthy, but they are not rich". When I asked him: "What's the difference?" he replied: "They are running away from poverty all the time and not moving towards happiness". He was absolutely right – and they were very rich but not satisfied and sometimes miserable! Very recently, I was fortunate enough to be in Gstaad, in the Swiss Alps, when I met a miserable multi-millionaire. During the course of our conversation, while he told me how unhappy he was, I asked him: "Why are you unhappy? You've got your health, your friends, you live in a beautiful place and you're obviously wealthy," and he told me: "I have a number in my head I want to achieve and I won't be happy until I achieve it!". When I asked him: "Why not be happy now?" he replied:

"I've got to drive myself." He was so fixed on his goals (and not his values) he was postponing his happiness until his bank account said a different number. So, let's now unlock the key to your happiness by working out what your values are and that will give you your definition of success to aim for. Whenever you visualise or think about your future, it's also important to always put yourself in the picture looking healthy, happy and successful too.

GETTING IN TOUCH WITH YOUR CORE VALUES

Remember, what matters to you are your core values and these are the bedrock of vision and success. These three questions will help you discover your values. By answering them in as much detail as possible, you will get a clear direction. Write your answers down so you can remind yourself of them. They may change over time and that's fine too.

What is most important to you in life?

Who are you when you're at your best?

How do you want to be remembered?

Clarity about your future

Now you've established your core values it's time to get even clearer about your future direction. These questions are deceptively simple but they will help you to gain further awareness and insight into what's really important to you.

They gradually become more complex as you work through them. In answering them you can gain not only clarity but also vision. You are priming yourself for success.

THE CLARITY PROCESS

 Grab a pen and answer the following questions.

Describe what it's like when your life is working well and you are operating at your peak potential or close to it.

What are your thoughts, feelings and behaviours?

What are your relationships like when you are in a state of peak potential?

continued

What are the results you achieve in your career when you are in this state?

Describe what it's like when your life is working well and you are operating at your peak potential to a five-year-old child.

Now carefully consider the answers to the following: If your life is the best it can possibly be...

How is your health?

How are your relationships when you are in your peak state?

How is your career?

How are your finances?

continued

How is your general level of happiness?

What would you like to celebrate this time next year in your peak state?

What has made your life work to date?

What will make you more successful over time?

Who are your advisors?

What are your key strengths?

What are your character traits that have helped you through tough times?

continued

If all goes really well, what will your life look like in five years?

Why is it that you want to accomplish the things you want to achieve?

Now you've completed the questions, while you are in this peak state of mind and body, squeeze your thumb and middle finger together and hold them together while you feel this good. Do it several times to create a strong associational link.

The definition of success

Now you have established your core values and differentiated them from your goals, it is time to answer the following question:

WHAT DOES SUCCESS MEAN TO YOU?

This is a very individual thing, as success means different things to different people. Take your time to really consider this question. Remember, any definition of success that doesn't involve you loving your life isn't a definition of true success!

When you get in touch with true success it will take the form of "I want to have a wonderful life that I love and it includes this, this…and this!" You need to think about relationships, how you feel and look, what you do…the list can be as long as you want. But a life that you *love* is a wonderful life. So simply saying "I want to be super successful in my business," or "I want to take over the world," doesn't take into account that the people who are super successful in their businesses or any other field often have done that by sacrificing a lot of things. If that worked for them, then great! But that might not be a wonderful life for you. Most of the people who chase Elon Musk's or Bill Gates' level of success actually would hate the reality of it.

Legendary jockey Frankie Dettori nearly died in a plane crash. But he bounced back from that defining moment in his life to embrace even greater success across his whole life. He recently won The Gold Cup for a staggering ninth time aboard Courage Mon Ami at Royal Ascot. But it's about much more than that. He once told me: "Since I had my plane crash in 2000 I decided a lesson [was] learned of life. I nearly lost my life. I could have broken more records. But I think I enjoy life more since then. I was 29 years old. I had a six-month-old child and when that plane was going down I didn't scream because I was actually disappointed. I was just disappointed it was over. I was going to die. When the plane goes down you think how many people survive? It was a miracle. For two years I couldn't sleep, I was low, I was depressed as I was trying to figure out why it happened. Then I said: "Records OK. They mean something. But really life is more important. I'm still doing my job, but now I'm doing it on my own terms." I truly believe Frankie harnessed his ultimate state of being and chose a life he loves in the aftermath of nearly losing it.

There are two very simple ways to tell if you haven't got the ingredients of your successful life quite right and you need to explore things a bit further. The first is that if your idea of success means your life is so busy that you would have no time for anything else, you need to have a rethink. Secondly, if you build your idea of success as the opposite of what you are afraid might happen in your future – for example you want control as you are running from chaos or you have the mindset: "I don't want to be this so I'm going to be that" – then you need to interrogate yourself further and think again. It's vital that your future success is built on positive foundations. So that means it should not involve running from negativity and fear.

If you aren't sure you've got it quite right, there is a really simple way to tell by how you are feeling. One of the ways to identify unhelpful definitions of success is there will be tension and a feeling of tightness in the body that comes with it. Whereas when you come to your functional definition of what success means to you there will be an expansiveness, an ease and a twinkly, inspired feeling and you will think: "Oh wow. Living that life really would be FANTASTIC!"

Turn thought into action

Now you've assessed your life, gained clarity about what success means for you, it's time to work out a plan of action. Have you ever had an idea for a product or service and months later you see that someone else has had the same idea and gone and done it? The difference between you and the person who created the product or service is that they did something about it! So, it's important to have not only a plan that excites you but to take action once you have it. Many people spend more time writing a shopping list than planning their life for the next five years. If you don't have a direction, it's like setting off into the ocean without a rudder and you could end up anywhere.

When I think about something I'd like to do in the future I have a particular process. I imagine what it's going to be like once I've achieved it and I notice what I will see, hear and feel. Then I work backwards, asking myself: "How did I get there?", "What will I have to do?", "What are the potential challenges along the way?", "How can I overcome them?" Planning can help you consolidate your goals, as well as calculate risks, anticipate problems, work out if it's something you truly want and trouble-shoot before you put your plan into action.

When I decided I wanted to be a hypnotist I did this process. It felt a bit scary and overwhelming as it was a huge leap from what I was doing, sitting on my own in a radio studio. I realised I would have to take some risks, educate myself about hypnosis and psychology, dress differently (my work uniform back then was jeans and a T-shirt), take some business risks, potentially risk losing money and potentially face failure along the way as I was stepping out of my comfort zone. I wasn't a natural stage performer, so I watched videos of people I thought were good and I would step into them and learn what it was like to be a confident performer and things about the way they talked to the camera and their stagecraft. I worked out a strategy including where I'd have to hone my skills and put in additional effort. I'd never really made a clear plan for my career before that moment. It was mind-blowing at the time, but I followed my plan and I changed my life. Now I want to help you do the same.

Creating your ultimate
state of being

Now I want to add the second state of clarity to your ulti-mate state of being using this deceptively simple process. I have used this throughout my career and I still do it to this day. Most recently I started an online hypnotherapy busi-ness with the largest online self-improvement company in the world, Mindvalley. I imagined we had the biggest and best hypnotherapy training in the world. I dreamed up as many details of how this venture would work as I could think of, what challenges we would face and how we would overcome them. I then back engineered the whole thing. I knew it would be successful but it has become even bigger than I had imagined. So now I'd like you to try it yourself.

CREATING A COMPELLING FUTURE

🔊 *Read through this technique before you do it.*
If you want me to guide you through it, download the
free audio at: paulmckenna.com/downloads

1　Imagine it's a year in the future and you have
had one of the best years of your life.

If that is true what must have happened with
*regard to your **health**, mental and physical...*
*your **relationships**, personal and professional...*
*your **career**... your **finances**... and your levels*
*of **happiness**?*

How does it feel to be living your values?
Which of your goals have you achieved?
Which ones have you made significant progress
towards? What new thinking and behaviours
have you practised? Who are you becoming?

continued

2 Now, imagine a cinema screen in front of you and on that create an ideal scene that represents all that you most want to happen in your positive future. Make sure you can see yourself in that future picture looking healthy, happy and successful. It can be realistic or symbolic (some people see a picture of themselves in a particular setting, looking a certain way – other people go for something more symbolic, like picturing clinking champagne glasses, celebrating a business deal, or a certificate of achievement on the wall).

Design your 'ideal scene' now. Where are you? Who are you with? Which successes are you most aware of? What do you like about it most? How happy do you look?

3   So, when you have made that image one year from now, make sure the image is big, bright, bold and colourful, the size of a cinema screen. You'll know you're doing it right because it feels really good just to imagine it.

4   Next, float back three months from your big picture and ask yourself what needs to happen three months before that to achieve your big goals a year from now and make a smaller picture that represents it. You may know straightaway, or you may just get a sense of what needs to happen. Make a picture that represents that.

5   Next, float back another three months from that picture and ask yourself what would need to happen three months prior to that?

6   Then, float back another three months from your last picture and ask yourself what needs to happen three months before that? And make a new image that represents that.

continued

7 Once again, float back three months from your last picture to now and then ask yourself what needs to happen from this day forward?

8 So, you are right back to now and you should be able to see a succession of images that show you the direction of your life over the next year. In all of them you should see yourself healthy, happy and successful.

9 Next, make all the images much bigger, brighter, bolder and more solid until they feel amazing.

You should now have a succession of pictures connecting the present with your positive, compelling future. The images should get progressively bigger with better and better things happening in them.

Look at those pictures and let your unconscious mind lock in the road map to your success over the next year.

continued

You should now be feeling very optimistic and motivated when you think about your future. It's important to do this process regularly and focus upon the future you want to have, look at your timeline and the succession of images of you succeeding and achieving.

Now, while you are in this peak state of clarity, squeeze your thumb and middle finger together and hold them together. Experience how fantastic you feel, let yourself live in those feelings and allow them to wash over you. Take as long as you need to do this. Do it several times to create a strong associational link.

By now you will be getting a sense for how different your life can be as you have stacked the super state of *clarity* as well as *self-belief* into your ultimate state of being. As you move beyond your old mindset and view of what you thought was possible your eyes will open to the amazing new world brimming with opportunity that you are stepping into. Each time you add a new super state your 'future self' is going to look different again. As you naturally begin to think of yourself as an even more resourceful, powerful person you will start to notice differences in your approach to life and other people may positively comment on the fact that you are different too. So, get ready for the next step in your transformation, because we are going to add the super state of *determination* to give you the drive and resolve to get you to where you want to be.

Chapter Three

Determination

While clarity and self-belief will get you so far, now we are going to add *determination* to your ultimate state of being. This mind/body state, which combines resilience, motivation and tenacity, will help you thrive when challenges inevitably come your way. As you build your inner resources it can help you to enjoy repeated success.

There are many great examples of determination leading to dizzying heights of success. One such example is that of Louis Pasteur, a microbiologist who became the father of immunology, invented pasteurisation to preserve foods, developed the rabies and anthrax vaccines and made a major contribution to combating cholera in his remarkable career. He once said: "Let me tell you the secret that has led me to my goal. My strength lies solely in my tenacity".

Everybody has determination – it's just that you may not be truly harnessing it fully right now. But we're about to change that. Its power should not be underestimated. My inner state of determination once saved my life. I have only ever had one moment where I truly thought "I'm going to die" and that was when I had a scuba diving accident in the '90s. I was on a dive abroad when I lost sight of my instructor and got caught in a powerful current. I was completely alone and I was dragged deeper and deeper. I kept trying to fight it, but it was futile. I honestly didn't think I had the strength to get out of it and it was the most terrifying experience of my life. I knew if I didn't get out of it, I'd run out of oxygen before I could reach the surface, so it was do or die. In that instant, something inside me went: "I'm not going to die this day" and I don't know where it came from, but I used every ounce of everything I had and found the superhuman strength to pull myself to the surface before my oxygen ran out completely. My determination combined with my survival instinct meant I lived. While not everyone will have an experience as dramatic as that, everyone will have a moment in their life where determination changes the path they are on.

Every comedian I have spoken to on my Positivity Podcast, has harnessed their super state of determination on their road to success. Without exception they have all had an experience where they've 'died on their bottom' on stage early in their career and were either heckled or nobody laughed. But while many would have thrown in the towel, the successful ones didn't. Instead, they tapped into their determination and talent before re-grouping and learning from the experience. Rob Brydon, who is one of the UK's most successful comedians, impressionists, a presenter, writer and award-winning actor is a great example of this.

Rob said there has been "all manner of gigs that were undignified, abject failures, dying on my bottom" in the early days. One South-east London comedy venue in front of a tough crowd was a defining moment for him. As he did a skit about growing up in Wales, a member of the audience started making sheep noises at him. He told me: "Then somebody else made a sheep noise. And then somebody else, like at the end of Spartacus. Before long, the whole room was making sheep noises. Inside my heart is racing, in my mind I'm running up and down corridors looking for something funny. Nothing came."

The venue's owner described it to Rob in the aftermath as a baptism of fire. It became a defining moment. Rob said: "As I drove home that night, I remember saying to myself: "Don't spend any more money as you have no future in this business." But the next morning I woke up and thought: "Right. I'll show them." I went back a few months later, and I didn't raise the roof, but they didn't make sheep noises." He said the secret to his success is: "I was tenacious. I didn't give up. I kept going. I think that's what makes the difference between those who succeed and those who don't. It's a trite old saying: 'a winner never quits'..." Determined people, like Rob, back themselves and they become winners in life. We can all do it.

The power of 'why?' in your future success

We are now going to build on the idea of what matters to you and what success means for you. When you visualise your future success, it's vital to consider the power of 'Why?' in order to strengthen your determination and ensure you are creating a truly meaningful, purposeful, happy and fulfilled future. There's a famous quote by philosopher Friedrich Nietzsche: "He who has a *why* to live for, can bear almost any *how*." So, knowing why you are doing it is critical. Nobody explains the importance of asking 'Why?' within the framework of your life better than business leader and author Simon Sinek. He says asking 'Why?' taps into the part of the brain that influences behaviour. He has analysed why certain companies or individuals become trailblazers or disruptors and what sets them apart. It has led him to create a concept called the golden circles. His three concentric circles make up three questions that everyone should ask. The innermost circle is 'Why?' the middle is 'How?' and the outer circle is 'What?' He says most companies know what they do, how they function and their USPs (their 'unique selling points'). In a recent TED talk Simon said: "Very, very few organisations know why they do what they do. And by 'Why?' I don't mean to make a profit – that's a result. By 'Why?' I mean: 'What's your purpose?' 'What's your cause?' 'What's your belief?' 'Why does your organisation exist?' 'Why do you get out of bed in the morning and why should anyone care?'" It works just as well for individuals as it does for organisations. You may know what you do and how you do it but if you now really analyse 'Why?' you can suddenly make a massive leap. It's important to not use 'Why?' in an umbrella way about your whole life. You need to look at specific elements of your life individually. So, for example, isolate relationships and career or it will fragment your thinking. Focus on one specific area at a time.

Simon says, instead of starting from the outer circle of 'what?' looking inwards, if you flip that perspective and start from the perspective of 'why?' and look outwards, it changes everything. So, while many people are very good at knowing *what* they do and *how* they do it, in terms of a motivation strategy for life, knowing *why* is critical. When you know *why* you become powerfully and purposefully driven. So, I know *what* I do as I'm a hypnotist. I know *how* I do it, which is through books, recordings, events and one-to-one coaching. But my '*why?*' is the bedrock upon which it's all built. My '*why?*' is because I feel compelled to help people, I'd like to change the world in some way for the better and I want to make a positive difference. Viewing my work through the lens of 'why?' has changed everything. It's the same when I think about my relationship with my wife Kate. The *'what'* is that we live together and we plan to grow old happily. I know *how* the relationship works but my 'w*hy?'* is that in sharing my life with someone who is my soul mate and for me is the perfect person and my favourite person in the world means that every day is a blessing. So, spend some time and work on your own 'whys?' to gain a whole new, empowered and beautiful perspective.

Here's an example of how someone with a career as a Producer might answer the questions.

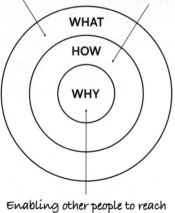

Organisation, communication, judgement and experience.

Creating an environment where people can flourish and guiding them along the way.

Enabling other people to reach their creative potential.

DISCOVER YOUR WHY

Grab a pen and fill in your own Why, How and What, opposite.

1   Pick an area of your life (such as career) and ask yourself *WHY* you do what you do by answering the following questions:

> What's my motivation?
> What's my purpose?
> What's my inspiration?

And write your answers in the very centre circle.

2   In the next circle write *HOW* you do it. What are the actions and processes involved?

3   Now in the outside circle write *WHAT* your products, services or results are.

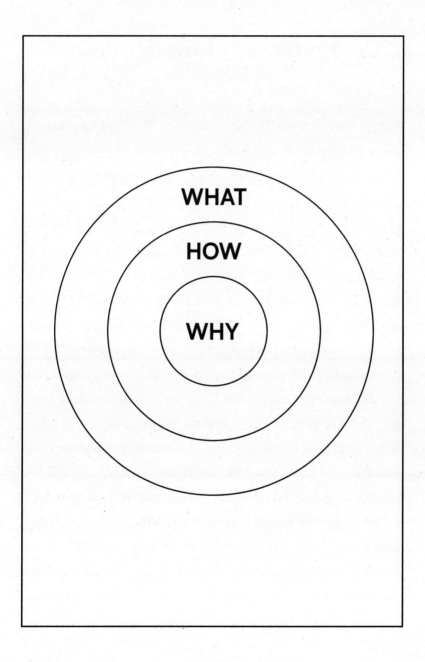

Determination breeds success

Failure can be turned into a positive. It is not necessarily a negative thing. Recognising that can change your whole perspective when things don't go your way, which is inevitable in life. There's a popular phrase in corporate training: "There's no such thing as failure, only feedback". Having determination can turn apparent failure into success – as long as you learn from your mistakes and don't give up. When I started out, I had a few things that bombed. One of them involved a doomed attempt at making an infomercial to share my self-improvement tapes with a wider audience. I could have wallowed in failure and given up on my dream, but I didn't. Even though things hadn't gone according to plan, I knew I had something that could really help people and that gave me the determination to keep going (I had combined my own values with my 'why?'). Life then presented me with an opportunity and I seized it. QVC, which had just started in the UK, got in touch and said: "Would you like to come and tell our audience about your self-help tapes on our channel?" I said, "Of course!" My failed infomercials were great training for that. As soon as I started talking, I knew exactly what to say! I was prepared to take knocks along the way, learn from my mistakes, but also I was primed to jump in with both feet when an opportunity presented itself as I had self-belief, and I was determined and clear that I wanted to share what I'd learned to change other people's lives in a positive way.

History is littered with people who had multiple failures before they succeeded. David Bowie's iconic career was preceded with four years of flops and knock-backs, yet he didn't give up. In 1965 his group The Lower Third failed an audition for the BBC's talent section, which was the quality control arm for performers. One judge described Bowie, then using his name David Jones as "an amateur sounding vocalist who sings wrong notes and out of tune". When he finally broke through with 'Space Oddity' in 1969, his legend was born. Thomas J Watson, the founder of IBM, famously acknowledged failure is part and parcel of the road to success. He said: "If you want to increase your success rate, double your failure rate." John Cleese has enjoyed a prolific and varied writing and acting career including *Monty Python's Flying Circus* and *Fawlty Towers* as well as roles in James Bond and the Harry Potter series. He recently posted online a rejection letter for *Fawlty Towers*, which said: "I'm afraid I thought this one as dire as its title. A collection of cliches and stock characters which I can't see being anything but a disaster". John wrote alongside it: "My greatest successes began with rejections". When I spoke to John about what keeps him going, he explained: "Some days when you are writing it doesn't happen. The only thing that keeps you sane is the knowledge that you can average a certain amount of work over a week and if you have a bad day there will be a better one coming up." So, creating a bigger context for failures and setbacks is also a part of a determined mindset. It can lead to astonishing success as his experience proves.

Bear Grylls, one of the most recognisable faces of survival and outdoor adventure and a former soldier in the British Special Forces has the ultimate determined mindset. He climbed Mount Everest after breaking three vertebrae in his back after a parachute accident; he circumnavigated the UK on jet skis, crossed the North Atlantic in an inflatable boat and climbed some of the most remote, unclimbed peaks in the world in Antarctica. He told me: "The universality we all have is the ability to fall down and get back up. It's how many times we can do that which separates people." Bear uses the carrot and stick mental approach. He says: "If you are in that situation and you're up against it and the rain is pouring down, or that mountain is steep in front of you, or the chasm is wide, or whatever that obstacle, whether metaphorical or physical is, if you are in it, you've got a choice. You either dig deep and you choose a positive attitude, you choose to be ruthlessly determined and to never give up. Or you have an alternative, which is to throw in the towel. Time and time again I've seen when people quit it's a short-term relief, it's a long-term pain.

So long as you're prepared from the outset to sometimes fail along the way, if you get knocked down seven times, and you're determined to get back up eight, then, you can make it.

Jump in!

Once you've strengthened your resolve there comes a point where very often you will have to take a leap of faith. Award-winning TV producer Mark Burnett has created a string of massive hits including *The Apprentice*, *Survivor* and *The Contender*. When I lived in America, we piloted a show together. He is the embodiment of the American Dream. He left Britain for a new life in LA in the '80s with £250 in his pocket and a great idea for a TV show. He worked as 'Manny' in childcare to make ends meet, then sold T-shirts on Venice Beach before becoming one of the biggest TV producers in the world. He has a mindset that he calls: 'Jump In', and we can all learn from it.

He says in his book: "Life is too short to be timid. So, if you have an idea, a passion, a belief – go ahead, jump in. What're you waiting for?" Mark practised his pitch with people before he hit the big time so he could get feedback and hone it. His strategy led him to write his book *Jump In!* - named after his mantra. He says far too many people wait until the timing is perfect and everything is the way they want it before they follow their dream. Mark wrote:

"It's about taking action. Nothing will ever be perfect, and nothing can be totally planned. The best you can hope for is to be about half certain of your plan and know that you and the team you've assembled are willing to work hard enough to overcome the inevitable problems as they arrive. Being calm and action-orientated in the face of difficult problems isn't taught in any MBA programme." So, it's all about a calculated leap of faith combined with resolve.

Finding resilience

While determination often involves 'toughing it out', resilience is also key. Many people think of resilience as the ability to 'bounce back' – but there's more to it than that. True resilience includes 'adaptability'. Being able to see things from a different perspective can give you an edge, as it enables you to think on your feet and be agile.

The Law of Requisite Variety tells us that the part of a system that has the greatest flexibility will always end up in control of that system. That can be a political party, a family, or a corporation. In simple terms, the person that is most able to adapt to an ever-changing environment is the most powerful. For example, as a hypnotist, if you have seven ways of resisting something, I need eight ways to help you. Among his many extraordinary traits, Mahatma Gandhi had supreme adaptability. He was famously agile as part of his negotiating strategy with the British Empire. He inspired millions to action but also masterfully negotiated one-to-one. It changed the course of history.

One of the most accomplished astronauts in the world, Colonel Chris Hadfield, who has flown three space missions, helped to build two space stations and commanded the international space station calls his extraordinary adaptability 'tenacious optimism'. He told me: "Things are going to go badly and things are going to go average and things are going to go well. My life is going to be dictated by how I respond to those three different sets of circumstances. Do it with as much gusto and fun and as well as you can. See where that takes you. That's my fundamental attitude towards life that has got me to the places I have been. To me, life is very much a mixture of what do you dream of, what are you capable of, how much you are willing to change and then see what you can accomplish." His traits, including supreme adaptability, have taken him to the stars!

Tap into your inner strength

As well as becoming adaptable, tapping into your core strength is hugely empowering. Have you ever noticed someone who, when facing a challenge in life, seems to find an inner resource, rises to the occasion and comes out of it stronger and better than before? Sometimes we underestimate what we are truly capable of, but we all have that grit within us. There's a famous story about Angela Cavallo who experienced a rare phenomenon called 'hysterical strength.' She summoned the strength of 10 men to lift a car off her child after he was pinned underneath it following an accident. In a similar case, Lydia Angyiou wrestled a 700lb polar bear in northern Quebec, holding it off in order to protect her son and his friends. These stories sound astonishing, but we all have that capability.

I once asked the legendary Olympian Roger Black, who has won a clutch of medals, and has gone on to become a successful motivational speaker, what was his winner's mindset. Remarkably, at 11 years old he was diagnosed with a heart condition and told he'd probably never be able to take part in competitive sport. Yet he went on to win

European and Commonwealth 400m titles and two silver Olympic medals. He said: "I didn't ever worry about what anyone else was doing. I decided I was going to simply run my perfect race." That determined, focused mindset is the difference that makes the difference.

One of the best methods I have found to help people find their inner power is The Aikido One Point Technique. Once you get the hang of it, you can use it anywhere, in any challenging setting. The way it works is when you think about a person or situation that is challenging, it throws you off balance. Examples are, for instance, public speaking, talking to your ex, or dealing with your boss. As Aikido is a defensive martial art, there is a big emphasis on being centred. Most people navigate life by talking in their own heads all the time, and making pictures and movies in their mind that aren't always helpful. But if you move your centre of attention to what Aikido calls your Hara, (which means 'making your will powerful') then you empower yourself. To do this, in your mind's eye, you need to move your brain (where all the negative movies and chatter is happening) to your tummy area. Then you visualise holding it there. Oddly, if I pushed you on your shoulder while you are doing this, I wouldn't be able to push you over as you become mentally *and* physically stronger.

AIKIDO ONE POINT TECHNIQUE

A quick note:

It can be useful to do this for the first time with the assistance of another person, but if you don't have anyone to do it with, you can always do it for yourself...

1 Stand up and think about a situation coming up in your life that you are worried or upset about. (This is not the time for major phobias – start with something relatively minor!) If you have someone working with you, have them push you gently on the shoulder. You will find you are very easily pushed off balance.

2 Continue thinking about that difficult situation. Give your discomfort level a score from 1 (at peace) to 10 (aaaargh!).

3 Now move your centre of attention from your head and put it in your stomach, put your attention on your 'One Point' – about an inch below your navel and roughly half-way between your navel and your spine.

This point is known in Japanese as 'hara' and in Chinese as 'tan tien', and is believed to be both the physical centre of your body and the central storage point for your 'ki', 'chi', or life force. Simply put, move your brain to your tummy and keep it there for now. If it helps, place one hand over that area of your stomach.

continued

If you have someone working with you, have them once again push you gently on the shoulder. You will know you are at 'One Point' when it is very difficult for them to push you off balance.

4 Finally, holding 'One Point' attention, think about the situation you were upset or worried about and notice the discomfort begin to reduce and drain away from 10 (or wherever it was on the scale) down to 1.

Again, if someone is working with you they can monitor your attention by pushing gently against your shoulder as you do this to make sure you are holding 'One Point'.

5 When you no longer feel discomfort thinking about the situation you were worried about, you can use your 'One Point' attention to mentally rehearse performing at your best. Feeling strong and resilient, imagine things going exactly the way you want them to. What will you see hear while you feel this

strong and in control. When you are actually in the situation, you can hold 'One Point' as you perform to ensure you will stay centred and peaceful throughout.

6 Now, while you are in this peak state of mind and body, squeeze your thumb and middle finger together and hold them together while you feel this good. Do it several times to create a strong associational link.

Motivation versus determination

There is a difference between motivation and determination. Determination is a notch up from motivation. Motivation is when we think: "I feel like I really want to go to the gym today," or, "I want to quit chocolate," or, "I want to lose weight." Determination is that moment when the cards are stacked against you and you think to yourself: "I'll show you". It's that moment when you decide: "I'm not going to stand for this anymore", or "I'm not staying in this dead-end relationship" or "I'm not going to stay in this job that's making me miserable" or simply "I've had enough". It's like a superpower of invincibility. The earliest memory I have of experiencing such a moment in my life was during my childhood. I have dyslexia and I was told in my school report: "You will never amount to anything". In that instant I could have been crushed and my life may have been very different. But I wasn't. Instead, I thought to myself: "I'll show you" and I have.

A while back I had a conversation with the king of motivation Tony Robbins, where we talked about how determination is the sum of more than motivation alone. We asked ourselves: "What is it that when people are told you can't, you won't, or you'll never amount to anything, that causes them to think: "Right, I'm going to prove you wrong." We concluded that the people who choose not to be crushed but instead tap into their determination and go: "Do you know what, I'll bloody well show you!" define the difference in human choices that makes all the difference in life.

Creating your ultimate
state of being

Now we're going to add the third super state of determination to your ultimate state of being. First of all, I want you to evoke it. So, if you won big on the lottery, would you be fussed about picking up your winnings? When you went for your first ever job interview that you really wanted, were you determined to do your best? When you met someone fantastic and thought: "I really want to date them," did you feel determined to win them over? When you found a cause you really believe in, were you determined to take action? If you answered yes to any of those questions, then you elicited the state of determination inside yourself. Because determination is a state of mind and body, I'd like to take you through a process called The Determination Switch that will enable you to shift into a state of intense focus and spring yourself from motivated to determined.

THE DETERMINATION SWITCH

🔊 *Read through this technique before you do it.
If you want me to guide you through it, download the
free audio at: paulmckenna.com/downloads*

1 Think about something you would love to
   be really determined to do.

2 Now, remember a time when you felt really,
   really determined in the past – a time when
   you took positive action. Fully return to
   it now – see what you saw, hear what you
   heard, and feel how good you felt.

3 As you keep going through this memory,
   make the colours brighter, the sounds
   richer, and the feelings stronger. Tell
   yourself to 'Go for it!' in your most
   confident inner voice!

continued

4   While you are feeling these good feelings, squeeze your thumb and middle finger together. From now on, each time you squeeze your thumb and middle finger together, you will begin to relive these good feelings.

5   Repeat steps 1 – 4 several times, adding in new positive experiences of determination each time until just squeezing your thumb and middle finger together brings those good feelings back up to the top and has you raring to go.

6   Still holding your thumb and middle finger together, think about that situation in which you want to feel more motivated. Imagine things going perfectly, exactly the way you want them to be. See what you'll see, hear what you'll hear, and feel how good it feels to get into action and make things happen.

7   Now, while you are in this peak state of mind and body, squeeze your thumb and middle finger together and hold them together while you feel this good. Pause, and take as long as you want in order to fully experience and remember the amazing feelings that go with it. Do it several times to create a strong associational link.

Now you've added determination to your ultimate state of being, along with self-belief and clarity there's no stopping you. Your future has changed for the better yet again. Take a few moments to visualise your life going forward from this place with more vision, confidence and mettle. Now it's time to add your fourth state of *connection*, which will help you engage with people and the world around you in a beautiful way.

Chapter Four

Connection

Everything (including you!) is connected. A great illustration of this is that if you have two pianos in the same room and you hit a C note on one, the other will also vibrate. It is called the Law of Sympathetic Resonance. But it's not just pianos and people that affect each other's frequency of vibration. Scientists claim that classical music and the reverberation of sound waves also makes plants flourish. A 2007 study by the South Korea National Institute of Agricultural Biotechnology showed plants reacted to classical music. More recently, in 2011, The Royal Philharmonic Orchestra released an album called *Music To Grow To*, based around similar research. It has been proven that plants that are played symphonies outgrow ones that do not, as it's thought the sound waves create a massage in the molecular structure.

Another amazing example of the connectedness of everything is illustrated by two studies that found orchestra conductors enjoy longer than average lifespans. According to Dr Dale Anderson, The Metropolitan Life Insurance Company once claimed conductors live, on average,

38 per cent longer than the general population. It led him to write a book called *The Orchestra Conductor's Secret to Health and Long Life!* Meanwhile, Dr Donald H Atlas also did research on the longevity of conductors, which was published in 'Forum on Medicine', a publication of the American College of Physicians. He felt it was driven by several factors including high intelligence, talent (or genius), motivation and most importantly, a sense of fulfilment that came with world recognition (living by their values). On the one hand, conducting an orchestra is great cardiovascular exercise, but one theory is their exposure to a wide range of frequencies means they *also* benefit from a kind of internal molecular massage from the frequency of sound that's resonating around them. So, music really is good for your soul! Sound is also a key part of the process I'm taking you on, via the hypnotic trance. Not only does trance relax you and let your body do its internal housekeeping, but when I'm training hypnotherapists, I always say to them: "Imagine you are bathing somebody in sound" – and that's what I'm going to do with you.

Connection is all about the links or associations we make with other things or people. It goes way beyond physical attraction and conversation. It is a universal phenomenon. We all have people with whom we connect. Think of falling in love at first sight, or your hackles bristling when a stranger you've never even met walks in, or meeting someone for the first time and knowing they are going to be a great friend. Think about connecting with nature as you walk through a park and how it lifts your mood. Rich people also tend to find each other, as do happy people – as the saying goes: "Birds of a feather flock together". But in the same way, unhappy people tend to be around other unhappy people as 'misery loves company'. The reasons behind it are complex, but one theory is that our brain works on a specific frequency of neurotransmission – a bit like a radio wave signal we are giving out. The thought is that people on a similar frequency will instantly connect with others on that same, or similar, frequency. At the same time, if we are emitting frequencies, that means there's an exchange of energy.

There is also a wealth of evidence for something called 'mirror neurons' in the brain. These are a type of brain cell that is activated both when someone performs an action and also when he or she observes someone doing the same thing. For example, when you see someone smile, your mirror neurons fire up, creating a sensation in your own mind of the feeling associated with smiling and that makes you smile too. It brings a whole new meaning to good vibes!

A vital part of connecting with others and the world is finding and harnessing a sense of purpose and meaning. Psychiatrist and Holocaust survivor, Viktor Frankl, who was held as a prisoner in four concentration camps, once said: "Purpose is the cornerstone of good mental health." Purpose can be many things. It could be becoming the best partner, parent or friend, tending a garden or even changing the world!

Connecting with others

Enhancing your ability to connect with other people is an essential component of your ultimate state of being as it empowers you, it also makes you feel good and it's essential to your sense of wellbeing. It also overcomes loneliness, which is an epidemic of our times. I've often heard people say: "I was in a room full of people and I have never felt so alone". What they are actually saying is they are not connected to them. Child prodigy William James Sidis is an example of this. He had the highest IQ ever recorded and is often called 'the smartest man in the world'. He's often cited as the inspiration behind the movie *Good Will Hunting*, although Matt Damon, who wrote and starred in the film, has never confirmed who it was based on. Sidis was the youngest person ever to go to Harvard at 11 years old and that year he delivered a presentation to the Harvard Mathematics Club. But because of his genius he struggled to connect with others and he rejected other people's expectations of him and his talents. He took a clerical job, and chose to live in obscurity, such was his sense of disconnect.

The impact of our connections on our wellbeing shouldn't be underestimated. Scientist Dr Matthew Lieberman used fMRI (frontal magnetic resonance imaging) which shows activity in the brain in real time, to demonstrate that our brain responds to social pain and pleasure in the same way as it does to physical pain and pleasure. Dr Lieberman has said: "The things that cause us to feel pain are things that are evolutionarily recognised as threats to our survival and the existence of social pain is a sign that evolution has treated social connection like a necessity, not a luxury." One way to think about this is if you ask someone about the most painful experience of their lives, it's likely they will tell you about the death of someone they love, not a physical wound. So, it is essential to invest time and energy into cultivating our connections as they are integral to our sense of wellbeing.

The three circles of connection

Now you understand the importance of connecting with others, it's time to look at your own social connections. This is something I have done myself and it was a revelation.

I am fortunate to have met many inspirational people in my life. Robert Evans, who is a legendary movie producer and studio mogul, taught me this process. He was the King of Hollywood in the '70s and he made *The Godfather*, *True Grit*, and *The Great Gatsby* to name a few. He was also a bit of a Hollywood maverick but he truly understood the power of being connected to the world around you. When I got a call one day to say: "Bob Evans would like to meet you", I was star struck! But we went on to become friends.

One day I told him that I was trying to decide whether to stay in LA or return to Britain and he told me the diplomat and former Secretary of State for the United States shared this simple process with him. He said: "Henry Kissinger told me you've got to make three circles. The first one is really big and that's your circle of acquaintances. The next one is smaller and that's your friendship circle. Then the smallest one of all is your *real* friends – the intimate circle of people who will be there for you and you'll be there for them no matter what." So, I went away and did it. I thought: "Crikey, I have been spending a lot of my time with acquaintances and not with my real friends because I was over-networking." For me, it was a major wake-up call. I realised I've got more real friends than I thought, but the majority were in the UK and Europe. I decided to move back to Britain there and then. As a result, I became much happier. I love this as it gets you crystal clear about the quality of your relationships with other people.

CIRCLES OF CONNECTION

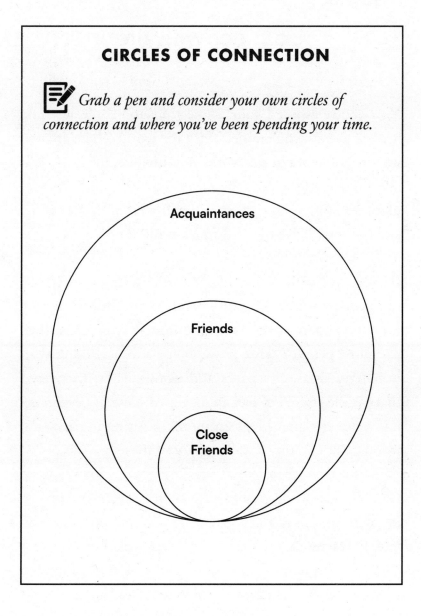 *Grab a pen and consider your own circles of connection and where you've been spending your time.*

Acquaintances

Friends

**Close
Friends**

Connect with life

Now you've assessed your connections to people, it's time to look at how you connect with the world. There are two ways to think about the world you inhabit. One is to see it as an unfriendly place. The other is to see it as a friendly place, bursting with opportunities. If you think of it as the latter, you will give out and *attract* positive energy.

Connecting with nature is one of the simplest ways you can boost good feelings. Researchers in Finland, led by Liisa Tyrvainen of the Finnish Forest Research Institute, measured people's sense of wellbeing and health in urban inner-city areas, city parks and woods. They discovered that people started to feel an increased sense of psychological wellbeing after just 15 minutes of sitting in parks and woods. Undertaking a walk enhanced those benefits.

Globally renowned chef Heston Blumenthal says connecting with nature is a key part of his life. He says: "I meditate, I exercise and it sounds really spiritual but it's not, I connect with nature. So, I'll notice the light shining off a leaf, maybe the wind on my skin and the smell. I've got a mountain bike, so I go off on pebbled tracks. When we live in cities we get bombarded with information. It's no wonder we get distracted. We are on a treadmill. It's hard to get off."

One of the ways in which I connect with life is to take a walk in nature every day with my Great Dane Misty and enjoy a sense of positive overwhelm by looking at the shapes, textures and colours of natural beauty. It never fails to lift my mood. So, from this point forward, whenever you get the opportunity, try to connect with nature for at least 15 minutes. Recognise the more you do it, the better you will feel. It will give you an instant boost!

Connect with everything

Now you've connected to yourself, other people, the world and life I am going to amplify those feelings exponentially. Astrophysicist Neil deGrasse Tyson recommends looking up to the sky and connecting with your place in the universe to give you a new sense of perspective. He told me: "When you look up, you are reminded that we are part of a much larger unfolding of cosmic events. And whatever might be the source of your sadness it will surely shrink in the context of earth as a planet. Just think about what the astronauts experienced and what we all experienced from the photos they took. Whatever were your problems on earth, they seem to evaporate in space."

Through the trance that accompanies this book, you can experience the ultimate feeling of connection. Buddhists and quantum scientists in some ways these days sound pretty similar. To radically simplify quantum mechanics, inside atoms and molecules are quarks and inside quarks is nothing. So, this poses the hypothesis that the universe is made of nothing and also raises the question some of the greatest minds have pondered – how physical matter gives rise to consciousness. Neuroscientist Professor Anil Seth of the University of Sussex has said: "The nature of consciousness is truly one of the great mysteries of the universe because for each of us, consciousness is all there is. Without it, there is no world, no self, no interior, no exterior. There is nothing at all." Questions like these straddle both science and philosophy.

If you think of everything around you – and yourself – as atoms and molecules vibrating at a density and frequency, it can open your mind to the idea that you are also a part of the sea of the infinite. At that moment, you are connected to everything. Zen Master Genpo Roshi is the creator of the Big Mind technique – a process where you connect with yourself, others, the world and the infinite. Years ago, it used to take years of meditation practice to achieve such states of consciousness, but now it can be done in minutes. Through Big Mind, you drop the idea of 'self' and 'other' in order to become part of the limitless sea of energy. This enables you to gain insights about yourself and your place in the universe. That is the ultimate connectedness, because in the infinite, everything is one. You'll have an experience of this when you use the hypnotic trance that comes with this book, where I do my own version of Genpo's Big Mind meditation.

Before you do the Big Mind trance, I want to stress that you should just relax into it and not overthink it. Often people say to me they can't focus or concentrate. Don't worry about that, as that's where I come in. Once I put you into the hypnotic trance, your mind will automatically become focused. When I was having my hair cut a month ago, the hairdresser told me: "Mindfulness and meditation is not for me as I can't focus." So, I asked her: "Do you think I should cut my own hair or should I let you do it?" She said: "Of course you should get a professional to do it!" I replied: "In the same way, if you want to get into a nice state of concentration, mental wellbeing and mindfulness you should let me do the work for you!". So, just sit back and relax and I'll guide you through the trance step-by-step and afterwards you will feel fantastic. After all, you don't cut your own hair or do your own dentistry or surgery, do you?

Amplifying your connections

Now you've connected with others and the world around you, it's time to amplify your connections even more. Connection is the secret to having (and keeping!) great relationships and living in a wonderful world. Music mogul Simon Cowell has an amazing ethos – and one of the cornerstones of it is that he really *listens* to people and cares about what they have to say. He truly understands the power of connection and the fact it makes the world a better place. He doesn't do it for any other reason than it makes him and the people around him feel good. His father taught him that everyone has a sign above their head that says "Make me feel important". Simon told me: "When you are making a show, for instance, you could have 500 people. That includes the person whose job it is to hold the door open for you. Most people will ignore those people and I hate that. I think it's rude. So, I try, when I'm in that situation, to be aware of what everybody's doing. As it all adds up to something successful." So, connecting with others means truly listening to what they have to say and giving them the space to say it. We've all had conversations where something else, such as a to-do list is running through our head and you aren't really focused to the point where you lose track. When our thoughts become an endless internal commentary, it's a distraction. It's important to try to be consciously present with the people around you. Wouldn't you expect the same from them? There's a great quote by author E.M. Forster which is the epigraph of the novel *Howards End* that says: "Only Connect". It's a great mantra for living.

There are endless ways we can connect with others to make the world around us a better place – even in unprecedented times. Best of all everyone benefits – including us! Throughout the Covid-19 pandemic there were countless examples of this. When I was watching the news one evening during the height of Coronavirus there was a feature on the epidemic of loneliness that was a devastating side effect of the pandemic. One artist who had lost his wife decided to connect with his neighbours in the block of flats where he lived through his painting. He put a letter through everyone's door asking if they would like him to do a portrait of them. His creativity created an opportunity for him to make new friends as they sat for him, outside and socially distanced. This is an example of something which became known as pandemic portraits. Artists across the world used their creativity to connect with others by painting them and in doing so not only did they create art and new social connections, but they also made the world a friendlier place!

This phenomenon wasn't just confined to painting. Professional photographer Tony Fisher from Derbyshire captured images of people, inspired by his own experience of loneliness. In the mid '90s he'd lost his wife and a short while later his parents died. His photographs, entitled 'Only The Lonely?' uplifted himself and others during Covid. Among the images he captured was something called The Belper Moo – another way people were connecting during Covid-19. Every evening at 6.30pm locals would stand on their doorsteps, or lean out of their windows to moo like a cow. While it was quirky, it brought people together as a community over 83 days. Pandemic choirs also helped people to connect around the world. They included the 'Sofa Singers' who gathered people to sing together online. Clapping for the NHS every evening in streets across Britain was also a part of this movement of connection. Not only did it show support for the National Health Service in the UK, but it was also the only time many saw any other people during lockdown. These all illustrate the endless ways we can connect with others to make our world a better place.

As well as giving you an emotional boost, there is also a physical reason why connecting with others makes you feel great. When you are in a like-minded group, be it a football match or a group meeting where you have something in common, you get a rise in serotonin – the happy hormone. Incredibly this can even happen when you are watching a hit TV show at home! There is a phenomenon associated with Event TV Shows – these are massive shows such as *Britain's Got Talent*, or a big football match on TV where millions tune in at the same time and share the viewing experience in real time. When you watch Event TV as it unfolds, your level of appreciation is higher than if you watched it on playback. This is because you are participating in an experience that connects you with others, even if they're not sat on the sofa next to you. Simply by knowing that millions of others are watching at the same time as you gives you a serotonin boost!

Creating your ultimate state of being

Now we're going to use an NLP technique to increase your sense of connection to people, the world and life and in doing so add your fourth super state of *connection* to your ultimate state of being. Through this simple visualisation process you are instructing your unconscious mind to make you feel more connected and when you feel it, every cell in your body will be oscillating on a frequency that allows greater connection. You will feel differently about other people, suddenly finding greater opportunities to connect with the right people and with the world. In turn, other people will want to connect with you.

ENHANCE YOUR CONNECTIONS

🔊 *Read through this technique before you do it.*
If you want me to guide you through it, download the
free audio at: paulmckenna.com/downloads

1   Remember times in the past when you felt connected with people, with the world, and with life.

2   If you can't remember a time, then simply think about someone who you believe finds it easy to connect to other people and the world and imagine stepping into them.

3   When you begin to get a feeling of being connected, give that feeling a colour in your imagination.

4   Now imagine spreading that colour up through your neck, into your head, all the way down through your torso and into your legs, until you are fully immersed in that colour.

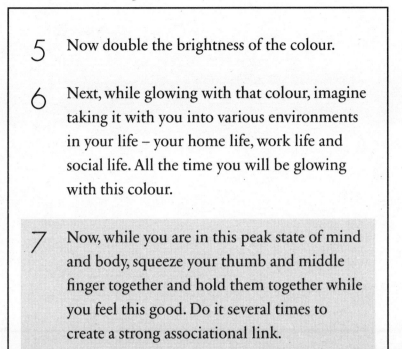

5   Now double the brightness of the colour.

6   Next, while glowing with that colour, imagine taking it with you into various environments in your life – your home life, work life and social life. All the time you will be glowing with this colour.

7   Now, while you are in this peak state of mind and body, squeeze your thumb and middle finger together and hold them together while you feel this good. Do it several times to create a strong associational link.

As you stack each super state together you empower yourself more and more. It will feel amazing. Take a few moments now to really absorb those great feelings. Once you've done that, you can continue to the next section where we will be adding the super state of creativity to take you even closer to your ultimate state of being.

Chapter Five

Creativity

You are either a creative person and you know it, or you are a creative person who hasn't realised it yet. Either way, this chapter will add a super state of creativity to your mindset and then stack it in your ultimate state of being. What people who think they aren't creative don't realise is that creativity has a structure. Once you know the structure, anybody can harness it. Creativity is a mind/body state, just like love, anger, apathy or optimism and that's why everybody has it. Even if you are convinced you are not a creative person, as you've been learning in this book it is possible to evoke the state of creativity either by remembering a time you experienced it or imagining what it would be like if you did. It's important to harness your creative brain as it will help you design a bigger, better and richer life for yourself.

The human mind is an awe-inspiring, inventive tool. Just think about all of the magnificent art, science, technology and concepts that people have dreamed up, using their creative mind. That's why it's an essential part of your new life. Successful people don't just create ideas or innovations, they also make a blueprint in their mind and then consider how to get it. They design their life. If you don't have ideas about your value-focused goals, if you haven't trained yourself to come up with ways to get there, or considered solutions if the road gets bumpy, then you are a passenger instead of being in the driving seat. Yet astonishingly, many people don't think of themselves as 'creative'. They assume you have to be a painter, poet or wear a bow tie and work in an advertising agency. However, it's important to realise that every undertaking requires a degree of creative thinking in one form or another. That's why we are definitely all creative!

Being able to think creatively will not only help you to design the big picture of your successful life but also the smaller undertakings within it. Years ago, I saw a fascinating interview with Sir Paul McCartney who had just written a ballet score called 'Ocean's Kingdom'. While he was already a creative genius, this was a new undertaking. One of his strategies was to imagine sitting in the theatre, watching the show and enjoying the finished performance in order to give him inspiration. He said in an interview at the time: "With most things I do, I imagine myself as someone in the audience, so I just thought: "Well, what would I like to see?" So, he tapped into his creative super state to design an entire experience for those who came to watch and a glitteringly successful show. What's even more remarkable is he was able to become involved in every part of the creative process from the characters to the plot and even some of the choreography during the collaborative process with renowned choreographer Peter Martins. That is the power of harnessing a creative super state to achieve beyond what you have accomplished before.

Creativity isn't just for artists and performers, however. Many people in business use creativity as a key ingredient of their success. Steve Wynn, an American mogul and billionaire designed some of Las Vegas' biggest casinos. He dropped out of the prestigious Yale Law School and went on to create the hugely successful Mirage, Treasure Island, Bellagio and Wynn Las Vegas. He used his creative super state to dream about 50ft volcanoes exploding in hotel lobbies and giant fountains that dance to classical music and he made them a reality within the field of business.

Steve told me he visualises and creates a casino inside his mind before he designs it in the real world – right down to the size of the space and the relationship of the objects, such as walls and furniture. He even imagines the ambience. If that's not amazing enough, he has an eye condition called retinitis pigmentosa and he is registered as legally blind. Steve may have impaired vision, but he's a man who has harnessed his creative vision within the field of business – and it's been his fortune!

I also harness my creative super state in all aspects of my life. I first started doing it when I used to do a comedy hypnosis show back in the '90s. One of my strategies was to imagine buying a ticket, walking into the theatre, sitting down and watching the show. By running every aspect through in my mind's eye, I could tell what was missing, what needed to be polished and what really worked. Today, I use a similar creative process when I'm writing a book. I imagine it, then I travel into the future and visualise myself holding it. At that point, I start to get a feeling of the tone of the book and its size. I do this several times during the course of writing it. As I get closer to completion, I am able to see it more clearly in my mind.

In a similar way, screenwriters often make a poster of the film they're writing, so they can look at it to gain inspiration. When I lived in Hollywood, I would often take one famous screenwriter off, in his imagination, to visualise watching the film he was creating. I'd get him to imagine the legendary film director Steven Spielberg was sitting next to him and offering his observations. When I go into corporations, sometimes they don't want me to use hypnosis, so we do something called 'strategic planning.' We sit in a group and imagine travelling off into the future and envisage how their product or service has developed, what their competitors are up to, and how the market has evolved in order to give them insight.

The fact that you may struggle with your creativity does not mean you are not creative. Remember, because creativity is a state of mind and body, the good news is that also means that you can tap into it. Even the most creative people in the world get blocked from time to time. But it's possible to not only spark creativity but also re-connect with it.

A few years ago, I worked with one of the greatest songwriters of all time, who would sit down at his piano in the morning to compose only to discover his creativity was blocked – it was the equivalent of writer's block. Then, later that evening, often when he had friends coming over, he suddenly felt the creative urge and he'd had to sit and compose there and then in case his fountain of creativity dried up again. It wreaked havoc on his work/life balance! He was living to work instead of working to live. Solving it was very simple. I had him go back to all the times when he'd written all his biggest hit songs and vividly remember what it was like. I asked him to give a name to this creative state and he called it 'the force', as he believed the songs were literally channelling through him. So, we created an anchor for 'the force'. Suddenly, at the tip of his fingers he had the capacity to tap back into his creative brain/body state and write hit songs on demand!

I previously mentioned that creativity has a structure. This was discovered by Robert Dilts, a brilliant author and NLP trainer. He used NLP behavioural modelling to explain how great, creative minds do the extraordinary things that they do. He modelled Walt Disney whose creative genius was combined with business acumen. He discovered Walt had three different mindsets whenever he was working on a concept. The first was 'the dreamer', who would conjure up limitless, amazing ideas in his mind. Second was 'the critic', who would brutally assess and critique these dreams. Third was 'the realist', who would look at what was left after the creative and critical process and decide what, if anything, was workable.

Dilts' model is far more effective than simply 'brainstorming' and it's something we can all use in our lives to interrogate our own ideas and dreams. It helps you to dream big, but also puts your ideas to the test in your mind and lets you try out different things, and you can use the same process to hone ideas as you work on them too. I find, as an author, I initially dream big and get my ideas down, then I critique what I've got, then I use that as a foundation to figure out what really works and what doesn't. Sir Paul McCartney also has a creative process, where he gets his initial ideas down and then hones it. When he was writing the classic song 'Yesterday', he knew he had a fantastic melody but at first he couldn't think of the right lyric. So, he sang 'scrambled eggs' until it came to him later in the creative process!

Creating your ultimate
state of being

Now you know that a well of creativity exists within you it's time to add that fifth super state to your ultimate state of being. I'm going to get you to remember or imagine being someone who is amazingly creative and get you to step into them. This will enable you to tap into a creative super state. We will then create an 'anchor', so that you're able to quickly access that state of mind whenever you need to. Let's do it now.

BOOST YOUR CREATIVITY

🔊 *Read through this technique before you do it.*
If you want me to guide you through it, download the
free audio at: paulmckenna.com/downloads

1   Remember a time when you felt creative
and you came up with a great idea or had a
flow of inspiration.

2   If you can't remember a time, then simply
think of someone who you consider to be
creative. It might be an inventor like James
Dyson, or Nikola Tesla. Maybe it's an artist
like Leonardo Da Vinci or Banksy. It could
even be your Aunty Gladys!

3   Next, either return to that time you felt
creative or imagine floating into your role
model.

continued

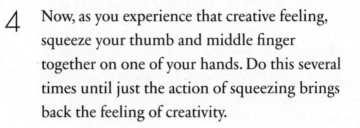

4   Now, as you experience that creative feeling, squeeze your thumb and middle finger together on one of your hands. Do this several times until just the action of squeezing brings back the feeling of creativity.

5   Now, while you are in this peak state of mind and body, squeeze your thumb and middle finger together and hold them together while you feel this good. Pause, and take as long as you want, in order to fully experience and remember the amazing feelings that go with it. Do it several times to create a strong associational link.

Now you've added the super state of creativity and stacked it into your ultimate state of being, along with self-belief, clarity, determination and connection, it will open your mind to the endless ways you can design your life going forward. Now it's time to add Energy and Health in order to take those great feelings and give them a massive boost!

Chapter Six

Energy and Health

We're just two steps away from your ultimate state of being. Now we're going to add the sixth super state of energy and health. Any decent biohacker will tell you there are four key things: sleep, diet, exercise and attitude that make all the difference in the world. So, this chapter will also show you what you can do to keep your body, mind and immune system as robust as possible. It includes specific visualisations focused around seeing yourself in an optimal state of health as well as insights to increase your sense of wellbeing through the rest of your life. Author, presenter and fitness coach Joe Wicks is someone who recognises the immense mind and body benefits of living a healthy life and he's sharing his message with millions. During the pandemic his online workouts helped boost the health and happiness of millions of people. He told me: "I know I'm a better human being when I exercise. So, if you are somebody who is sedentary who finds it difficult to get your mind into exercise, just know it's not about weight loss, it's more than that. It's going to change the way you feel and you are going to live a much happier life."

Even though medical advances have eliminated many diseases, as we get older, many of us get sicker. There are steps everyone can take to avoid preventable illnesses in later life. Healthy-ageing researcher and Professor Dr Norman Lazarus once described by the *Sunday Times* as "the octogenarian professor who holds the secret to eternal youth" says simple, but strategic changes can make an extraordinary difference. In his book *The Lazarus Strategy: How to Age Well and Wisely* he says: "The decision of how we age... is in our hands." He says that research has proven that many diseases are actually largely the result of lifestyle choices people have made, rather than what ageing does to us. In your 40s and 50s, simply getting active (if you aren't already!) will keep you healthier. He advocates a carrot and stick approach. Even though some people don't like doing it, the fear of what you could lose (optimal health) is the stick that should spur you to get moving to protect it (the carrot).

Professor Lazarus says three key behaviours are the difference that makes all the difference. He says one way to think of them is like a red, white and blue flag, split into equal thirds. The red third represents *exercise*, while the blue third represents *healthy eating* and the white third represents *good mental health*. His model says if you are ageing well, then the three parts of the flag will shrink in size evenly (this is because a bit of decline is part of the natural ageing process). But he warns: "However, if you are sedentary, often overeat and are perhaps slightly downhearted, then the three colours are certainly out of kilter." When those three sections of behaviour are out of sync, then healthy ageing won't happen.

Recently Vincent Dransfield from New Jersey, USA, reached the grand age of 109 years old. Incredibly he still drives, runs errands and lives independently and he credits his long and healthy life with remaining optimistic (mental health), staying active (physical health) and good food (healthy eating). Whether he realises it or not, he is living by the Lazarus goals for ageing well. The three parts of his flag are all in harmony, so Vincent is ageing in a truly exceptional way. We should all aspire to it.

The importance of your immune system

Most doctors agree the mind has a massive effect on people's sense of wellbeing. Work continues to understand whether hypnosis could have a more significant role in conventional medical treatments of the future. There is a field of science, known as psychoneuroimmunology (PNI) where psychology, neurology and immunology meet. My interest in this area began 25 years ago when I read about a doctor who hypnotised couples who couldn't get pregnant yet there was no biological reason why. Amazingly, 50 per cent of them went on to have babies!

Armed with this knowledge, I agreed to help a lady whose immune system attacked her foetuses so she couldn't carry a baby to term. It was a heart-rending case. She told me: "I'll try anything". Her husband didn't believe a word of it. I also explained: "I honestly don't know if this will work or not. But I'm going to do my best for you." I got her to talk to her doctor so they could explain, in simple terms, the process of what would happen if the fertilisation of her baby happened normally and her immune system protected the foetus. The aim was so that she could visualise her entire, healthy conception, pregnancy and smooth, successful birth like a movie in her mind. Once she did that, I then got her to move that movie literally into her womb using visualisation. I then told her to run it four or five times a day. Within *weeks* she fell pregnant and later gave birth to healthy twins. It was a magical moment in my career. I have gone on to help seven couples – and three of them had twins! It's amazing how times have moved on, as 25 years ago this type of work was hugely controversial. Today if you Google: "Can your immune system be affected through visualisation?" study after study says yes it can.

Other research has shown how the power of visualisation can affect your health. Two doctors at the Yokohama City University in Japan showed that 84 per cent of volunteers could stop their body's allergic reaction to poison ivy using visualisation. The itching, swelling and blistering vanished when the people went under hypnosis, and simply imagined the poison ivy to be a harmless plant. Even more interesting, many of them broke out in blisters when they reversed the experiment and got them to imagine a harmless plant was poison ivy!

Psycho-oncology also looks at body and mind interactions in cancer patients. Dr David Spiegel has led pioneering research on the effect of psychosocial treatment on survival rates of 86 patients with metastatic breast cancer. His study, in 1989, involved half of the patients all receiving the latest medical treatment. The other half also received the same cutting-edge medicine, but they also learned simple self-hypnosis and had group therapy sessions. In that pioneering study, when they looked at the survival rates after 10 years, they found the second group had lived, on average, twice as long as the first. Of course, nobody is saying that hypnosis is a cure for cancer. But there is on-going research into how it could improve the quality of patients' lives. At the beginning of the pandemic, I put up my Radiant Health trance for free on my YouTube channel and invited people to use it to help boost their health. So far, it's had 300,000 listeners.

The extraordinary power of the mind

Through my work I have helped soldiers and paramedics to overcome Post Traumatic Stress Disorder, caused by the horrors they'd seen. I have also helped people who were deemed to be 'untreatable' by others in the medical profession using the power of their mind to improve their health in some way. My most extraordinary case was that of a carpenter called Ray Mash who suffered from a super rare condition called 'hysterical blindness' for eight years. Doctors could find no physical reason for his blindness, but nonetheless he couldn't see. Ray's story illustrates just how deeply the mind and body are interconnected. Doctors told him part of his brain had switched off and they couldn't get it back. Ray's case was so unusual – it's like finding some extinct species of animal when you are a biologist. Over the course of a year, I was able to help him. I talked directly to his unconscious mind in order to build new neural networks. The brain has plasticity so when you injure parts of it, other bits can learn to do what those damaged bits once did. So, through a variety of processes, I got him to visualise himself as someone who could see again. When I started, I honestly didn't know if I could help him, but over a period of months, Ray got his sight back. Some doctors theorised I'd somehow repaired the neurological damage. My theory is that his brain got used to not seeing. By tapping into both his conscious and unconscious mind, we somehow rebooted it. The magical moment for me was when he saw his wife Karen's face for the first time in nearly a decade. Since then, he's even driven a car! Ray gave his blessing for me to share his story to illustrate how the brain and body are inextricably linked.

I also worked with a lady with cancer to help her immune system bounce back during her chemotherapy treatment. Each time she had a round of chemo her immunity became depleted. So, I set about building an *immune system booster* with her. This is a simple visualisation technique to promote healing. Her doctor told her that it usually took 10 to 14 days for her body to return to normal after the type of chemotherapy she was having. However, I got her to visualise her immune system going into overdrive in order to help it bounce back quicker. The way it worked was she imagined a blue light glowing on her left arm. She'd then visualise this blue light spreading out around her entire body, signalling to her unconscious to boost her immunity. When she started doing this several times a day, her immune system shot back to normal after five days. Her doctor could hardly believe it. I want to stress that I couldn't do anything to cure her cancer. But her quality of life improved. What gave me the idea was an experiment carried out with children in Minnesota. The children were shown a videotape featuring puppets which represented the immune system at work. One puppet represented a virus, while another one (which looked like a police officer) represented the immune system working at its peak. In a sense, the video was a piece of software; a simple model for the internal workings of the body that the children could easily understand. But here is the really incredible part. When the video was over, the children were told to close their eyes, relax and imagine more police officers in their bloodstream. Samples were then taken from each of them and when analysed, the results showed their levels of antibodies had rocketed. Their immune systems had kicked into overdrive as though they were fighting off real infections, just by *thinking* about it.

This astonishing study spurred me to keep wading through the clinical research and I discovered similar experiments – for example, the work of physician Dr Emmett Miller M.D. who also uses guided imagery to boost people's immune systems. He'd created a video of a trance using hypnosis

to promote healing. The video had cartoon-like characters that resembled white blobs to illustrate things called
macrophages, which are critical for regeneration. Another
blob represented killer T-cells floating through the bloodstream, wiping out invaders. Similar to the experiment in
Minnesota, his visualisation trains the immune system to
work optimally. So, I decided to try it on myself. I chose
to visualise a control desk with a computer screen. To acti-
vate it, I push a button marked: 'Immune System Booster'
and I visualise toxins being cleared, rogue cells taken away
and my entire system operating in equilibrium. The result
is that I haven't had a cold in five years and I used to get one
every few months.

In the trance that accompanies this book there is a special
section where I'm going to ask your immune system, via
your unconscious mind, to work perfectly. I'm also going to
help you to build your own immune system booster and I'll
instruct your mind and body to work in greater harmony.

The importance of tackling stress

Tackling stress is also critical for optimal energy and health. I believe that the major threat in modern life is being attacked by our own fight-or-flight internal defence system being triggered too often. So, in order to live your best life, you need a strategy to manage stress. Our ancestors needed extreme physical reactions and a burst of energy to enable them to fight a wild animal or run away. When the mind perceives a threat, the heartbeat quickens, the pupils dilate, muscles tighten, adrenaline courses through the bloodstream, the digestive process halts, blood pressure rises and the immune system is suppressed so that energy can be directed elsewhere. This is known as the fight-or-flight response. However, the problem is today we are continually preparing for emergencies that never happen. Driving to work there's a traffic jam or you get into an argument, you receive an unexpected bill, the kids have made a mess, or you are criticised. These things may not seem like threats to you, but your nervous system can't tell the difference between a physical threat to yourself and a threat to your ego. So, if someone criticises you, your mind responds to the situation with a stress response that produces toxic chemicals in your bloodstream. It is important to have an emotional dynamic range, as if someone is attacking you, then you need to get angry to defend yourself. But if the stress response is being unnecessarily aroused all day long, that builds up over time, causing problems, because your health is affected by your thoughts.

The Covid-19 pandemic also triggered a psychological pandemic where stress levels rose to unprecedented levels. Many people are still experiencing the repercussions of that around the world. We all need a certain amount of stress as it actually *motivates* us to do things like get out of the way of an oncoming car (you could describe this as positive stress). But the continual *inappropriate* triggering of stress in our mind isn't good for us. So having a strategy to keep stress as low as possible will ensure it doesn't take an unnecessary toll.

Your ultradian rhythm

Another simple and highly effective way to manage background stress is to harness the natural system we all possess in the Ultradian Rhythm. Recent research has shown that the mind and body have their own pattern of rest and alertness with one predominant cycle that occurs approximately every 90 minutes. This is when the body stops externally oriented behaviour and takes about 15 minutes to relax and replenish its energies. It's those moments when you find yourself daydreaming and a gentle, sweet, soft feeling is present in your body. It's quite simply the body's own natural stress control mechanism. Unfortunately, many people override this message from their body that it's time to relax a little. Instead, they have another cup of coffee, or they try even harder to concentrate. After a while, they establish a pattern of overriding their natural rhythm. In future, whenever you find yourself daydreaming and a feeling of comfort starting in your body, if it's appropriate, allow yourself to really relax for 10 to 15 minutes. Go with it. Give yourself a break because you will rouse up feeling refreshed and you will be more productive!

The importance of
rest and recovery

Some years ago, Virgin Atlantic asked me to do an experiment in a busy shopping centre where people were able to step into a booth where I hypnotised them in just 25 minutes to believe that they'd been on a relaxing, two-week holiday in the Caribbean. The results were fantastic! People emerged from the booth, happy, relaxed, raring to go and in some cases, looking younger as their stress wrinkles had melted away. A number of journalists also took part in this experiment and the result was it became an international news story. This illustrates how taking rest and recovery time are crucial to attaining a peak level of performance and it boosts your energy levels too.

So, while this may surprise you, in order to give you more energy, we are now going to add *relaxation* into your ultimate state of being. Rest and sleep have been proven to have a positive effect on the immune system and it allows us to recharge. Most ultra-achievers are bursting with energy, yet they don't burn out because rather than treating life as a marathon, they think of it as a series of sprints with recovery time. This is also the difference between being enervated and energised. Being enervated means you have a combination of tension and energy, which can run too hot and burn itself out. Most people's sense of what energy feels like is an enervated state. This ultimately hampers performance.

So, I'm going to help you attain a relaxed, alert, 'energised' state that means you can have more mental and physical resilience. Being energised is all about tapping into your flow or chi (where the natural, limitless, energy of life and creativity bubbles up inside you like a spring). This keeps you at the top of your game.

Self-hypnosis

Practising self-hypnosis is a good way of giving your mind and body a deep way of relaxing and an instant energy boost. You will emerge from it as if you have recharged your batteries. To achieve this state, I often relax into a trance where I imagine myself sunbathing on an exotic beach. Given that the nervous system doesn't differentiate between a real and a vividly imagined event, when I awaken from it, I feel as though I've just been on holiday. As far as my nervous system is concerned, *I have!*

So now I'd like to introduce you to The Ultimate Power Nap that you can do once a day to recharge your batteries and enhance your energy and wellbeing. Only do it when you can safely relax completely. The more you practise this technique, the more effective it becomes. Make a point of doing this every day. It doesn't take long and it's a good habit to establish. You don't have to make an announcement before you start. If you do it on the bus or train, people will think you are just dozing. Don't attempt it while driving or operating machinery.

SIMPLE SELF-HYPNOSIS

🔊 *Read through this technique before you do it.*
If you want me to guide you through it, download the
free audio at: paulmckenna.com/downloads

1   Imagine how you would look if you were
    twice as relaxed as you are right now.

2   Imagine floating into that more relaxed 'you.'
    See through the eyes of your more relaxed self,
    hear how it sounds and feel how it feels to be
    twice as relaxed.

3   From this place imagine how you would look
    if you were twice as relaxed again as you are
    right now.

4   Imagine floating into that more relaxed you.
    See through the eyes of your more relaxed self,
    hear how it sounds, and feel how it feels to be
    twice as relaxed.

continued

5   From this place imagine how you would look if you were twice as relaxed once again as you are right now.

6   Imagine floating into that more relaxed you. See through the eyes of your more relaxed self, hear how it sounds, and feel how it feels to be twice as relaxed.

Creating your ultimate state of being

However your health is currently, this technique is designed to help you reinforce your overall wellbeing.

ENHANCE YOUR WELLBEING

🔊 *Read through this technique before you do it. If you want me to guide you through it, download the free audio at: paulmckenna.com/downloads*

1 Imagine a cinema screen in front of you.

2 On that screen see a movie of you in perfect health.

3 Notice your posture, the expression on your face, the light behind your eyes and the glow of radiant health and strength that you have.

continued

---

4   Look at every detail and notice everything that lets you know that you are healthy.

5   Now float over and into that super-healthy you.

6   See the world through the eyes of your super-healthy self, hear your internal dialogue saying, "I feel healthy, I feel great!" and feel how it feels to feel super-healthy.

7   Now notice where you feel the best feeling in your body and imagine giving it a colour.

8   Now imagine moving that colour all the way up to the top of your head, down through your shoulders, chest, legs and all the way to the tips of your toes.

9   Now double the brightness of the colour and then double it again and double it again until you are glowing with this healthy feeling, radiating it through every cell in your body.

10 Now, while you are in this peak state of mind and body, squeeze your thumb and middle finger together and hold them together while you feel this good. Do it several times to create a strong associational link.

Now you have harnessed your super state of health and energy and stacked it with self-belief, clarity, determination, connection and creativity into your ultimate state of being. Notice once again how you feel and let the great feelings wash over you for as long as you need. You are now within touching distance of your ultimate state of being. Now it's time to add the icing on the cake by adding the final super state by reconnecting with your inner happiness.

Chapter Seven

Happiness

This final chapter is different. Instead of asking you to *find* the seventh super state of happiness in order to add it to your ultimate state of being, I'm going to ask you to *reconnect* with it. There are two different approaches to happiness. One theory says that happiness is innate. The second theory says that there are external things that can make you *happier*. The reason traditional thinking says that external things will make us happier is that we most easily access that feeling with certain people or in certain situations. But the latest thinking is that actually we can experience happiness with anyone or anywhere as it already exists within us and it's been a part of our being since birth.

Social researchers have measured happiness levels in Europe and the USA and they have not significantly increased since the 1940s. So, in the past 80 years, while we have become healthier, live longer, have better medicine, housing and communication, and live in a comfort-driven culture, the research shows we are no happier in the developed world. This is partly due to the distinction between happiness and pleasure. Pleasure is enjoying a bubble bath or buying a new item of clothing. Happiness is when we live by our values – remember, they are the things that are most important to us. If happiness was determined by pleasure, then people with the most money would be the happiest and that's not the case. In one study, the richest people in America in the Forbes 400 were found to be no happier than the Masai tribespeople in East Africa.

Recently I helped one unhappy super achiever who had phenomenal career success, which was a source of pleasure, but felt that somehow real happiness was eluding him. When he was in trance, I got his unconscious mind to go on a search and find the elements in his life that were essential for happiness. He came out of the trance glowing. What actually took place was his brain had showed him many happy times from the past, which included, for example, a relaxed experience in the garden when he was playing and laughing with his children, amongst other memories. His mind noticed a collection of elements such as the peaceful environment, intimacy with loved ones, absence of stress, connection to nature, and moving forward, his mind would take those building blocks and search to create new experiences based on those elements. Just as there are only seven notes in music, but millions of beautiful songs can be created from them, in exactly the same way, his brain was reconfigured to notice on a wider scale where there was joy, beauty and happiness and to go on a search to create more happy experiences. When you listen to the hypnotic trance, we're going to do the same thing. We're going to get your mind to search and sort for the essential elements that make you happy, so you can create even more happiness in your future.

Happy people

Now it's time to focus on finding ways to reconnect with your inner happiness. We all have people around us with whom we can most be ourselves and with whom we feel happiest. Those people aren't the external cause of our happiness, but they are people with whom it's easier to access the happiness within us.

The 80/20 audit, which is also known as the Pareto Principle, asserts that 80 per cent of outcomes come from 20 per cent of any given effort. Vilfredo Pareto found that when he was harvesting peas in his garden, 80 per cent of the peas came from 20 per cent of the pods and he wondered if this principle held true in other areas and generally it does. For example, 80 per cent of the money you make comes from 20 per cent of your effort. 20 per cent of your carpet is walked on 80 per cent of the time. In the same way, 80 per cent of the happiness you enjoy will be accessed from being with 20 per cent of the people you know. Conversely, 80 per cent of the misery and angst you experience will come from 20 per cent of the people you spend time with. So, an audit can help you to spend time with those who lead you to access your inner happiness the best! When you do something repeatedly (like access your inner happiness!) you also reinforce it. So, that automatically makes you even happier!

Being happy makes the world around you a happier place. The founder of Mindvalley, Vishen Lakhiani, is someone who inspires people to tap into their happy state. He says one of his golden rules in life is whenever he goes into a room, he always thinks to himself: "How can I lift everyone up?" When you see him speak at events, the room goes wild and even when he turns up to dinner, the energy in the room bumps up and you find yourself laughing more and feeling boundlessly optimistic. His happiness, enthusiasm and love of life make it easy for people around him to access their own great feelings. You could say it's infectious!

So, even though this sounds a bit ruthless, I'd like you to do an audit. One way to exercise the 80/20 rule is to flick through your phone and ask yourself: "Who takes my energy up?" and "Who takes my energy down?" Some people will take you down only on occasion as they need you to help them through a bad patch. They don't count for the purpose of this process as that's not the same as people who repeatedly drain you and are energy vampires.

So, you need to pinpoint the ones who continually leave you feeling drained and decide to spend less time with them. Then work out who the people are who lift you up, make you feel good and make it easier for you to access your inner happiness. Then make sure you spend *more* time with them. That's the conscious bit.

But the really cool thing we are going to do in the hypnosis is I'm going to say to you: "I want your unconscious mind to bump your inner happiness levels up and go and seek out more of the things that will enable you to access those good feelings. That will install a backdrop of happiness like a positive computer program that will help you feel better than ever before!

Happy places

As well as working for people, the 80/20 principle works for the places where you access your inner happiness most easily. Think of them as your happy places. Ask yourself: "Where makes me feel happier?" You can choose as many places as you like. It could be sea and sunshine, pottering in the garden or spending time with family. Once you isolate them you can focus on spending more of your time there. While we all have to work, you can consciously immerse yourself in your happy places when you have free time.

In the flow of happiness

Another way to access your inner happiness is to get 'in the flow' with something you love doing. That can be work, a hobby or a fun pastime! You have already accessed your flow of energy in the Health and Energy section. Now, through the trance that accompanies this process, we're going to take the flow through all aspects of your life. Psychologist Mihaly Csikszentmihaly found that when you are in a 'flow state' you enjoy an optimal experience and productivity in what you are doing. What's interesting is that the person experiencing what you create enjoys your flow, too. That's why poetry, music or a painting can uplift us.

Why happiness is inside us all

Too many people spend their days endlessly seeking out happiness or trying not to lose it. One of the world's leading success coaches Michael Neill says that's where we've been going wrong. He says:

"Wellbeing is not the fruit of something you do; it's the essence of who you are. There is nothing you need to change, do, be or have in order to be happy."

Michael's take on happiness is that you are not broken and you don't need to be fixed as your natural, default state is one of happiness. He says, as you've discovered, that while it's easier to feel happy with certain people or in certain situations, actually happiness can happen anywhere. In his book *Supercoach*, Michael says: "Happiness leads to success. Wellbeing leads to inspiration. Success and inspiration become the basis for an ever more wonderful life." Yet most of us have the misconception that life is based on a sliding scale where at one end there's happiness and at the other end there's misery. Due to that fundamental misunderstanding, we expend huge amounts of time and energy trying to attain happiness, keep it, or not to lose it by changing the world around us but happiness isn't a goal to be achieved (or lost). It's actually already there and it has been since we were born.

A baby's default state (when they are a blank canvas uncluttered by childhood conditioning) is one of pure, gurgling happiness and contentment. It's only when that bliss needs feeding, burping or a nappy change that this state is interrupted and then, of course, they scream the place down! But when the baby is given food, a change or a winding, more often than not, that blissful state returns. Over time that baby loses sight of the fact that its natural state is one of happiness as it confuses those interventions as being the external cause of its happiness. This sets us down the wrong path of chasing happiness for life! But once you remember that happiness is something that existed within you all along, your perspective changes. Michael says: "Happiness is right here, right now, and there's nothing we need to do, achieve or change as it's already within us." So, when you change on the inside then everything on the outside changes, too. Michael says: "Once you reconnect with your happiness you are *happily achieving* instead of *achieving to be happy*."

Embracing your natural state of happiness doesn't mean there won't be obstacles and hurdles along the way. However, happiness will remain the backdrop to your life even in difficult times. Spiritual teacher Eckhart Tolle says you can be the most enlightened master, the most spiritually cool person but it doesn't mean you aren't going to have challenges. He says: "The only difference is, as you awaken spiritually the way in which you respond to the challenges changes. And that is all-important. How you confront the challenges of life, how you react to or respond to the challenges of life determines how you experience your life."

His take is it's not so much what's going on in the external world, it's what's going on *inside you*. Eckhart says: "The primary cause of unhappiness is never the situation but your thoughts about it. Be aware of the thoughts you are thinking. There is the situation or the fact and here are my thoughts about it." He says when you recognise the thoughts are merely your perceptual filter, everything changes. So, whichever way you look at it, happiness is an inside job.

Choosing to embrace inner happiness

If you need further proof that happiness already exists within us, a recent happiness survey asked 1,000 people if nothing in their lives changed, (such as job, home, etc.) could they still be happy. A massive 95 per cent of people said YES. This tells you something really important; that tapping into your innate happiness is a CHOICE. So, let's choose to experience more of it! That is as simple as harnessing the power of your mind and thoughts. I am sometimes asked what is the single most important thing I have learned through the years and it's this;

YOU GET MORE OF WHAT YOU FOCUS ON.

So, the more you focus upon your inner happiness, the happier you will become! Happiness is a neuro-chemical event and so thinking about good stuff (and doing things or spending time with people who allow you to access it easiest) will increase your serotonin, dopamine, endorphins and your happy neuro-transmitters. You will be in a mind/

body happiness loop! This will help you to make happiness the backdrop to your life.

There's a common misconception that happiness is being 'up' all the time – it's not. Happiness is like the background music. It doesn't mean we still won't experience emotional pain, fear, anger or any of our other emotions. Remember, it's important to have a full dynamic range of emotions to lead a functional life. The purpose of fear is to say 'be prepared', if there's a threat to our physical self or reputation, that feeling of fear is there to protect us. If somebody violates one of our standards and is, for instance, rude to us, we get angry and tell them to stop. If somebody we love leaves us, we feel sad because we miss them. If we didn't experience all of these emotions, we would not be able to have any sense of value. So, in turn we wouldn't understand what true happiness is. However, we don't want to live purely in negative feelings as if all our bandwidth is taken up with them there's no room for the positive ones, including love, joy and passion.

Your gratitude journal

Keeping a happiness and gratitude journal is also a fantastic way to reinforce your positive, happy life. If you start with being grateful for your health and family, and also the smaller things like the first cup of tea in the morning then you are setting yourself up to feel good for the rest of the day. These simple actions reinforce happiness in your unconscious mind. It also tells your unconscious: "Give me more of that". A gratitude journal is also a great tool when you are feeling a bit down, as it can remind you of what you have, instead of what you don't. I've included a gratitude journal at the back of this guide to start you off.

Creating your ultimate state of being

Now let's harness your super state of happiness and add it to your ultimate state of being. Years ago, I sat doing this NLP technique remembering happy times, getting the feelings, living in that happy moment and visualising how it would feel to be truly happy in all aspects of my life. I made myself so happy that when I went out to pick up a pizza I walked into the takeaway and ecstatically said: "I'm here to pick up my pizza!" with a beaming smile on my face. The guy behind the counter huffed: "What are you so happy about?" And I said: "Absolutely nothing!" He spluttered: "What?" And I replied: "Yep, absolutely nothing. I just made myself happy and it feels absolutely terrific." So, let's do that with you right now.

INCREASE YOUR HAPPINESS

🔊 *Read through this technique before you do it.*
If you want me to guide you through it, download the
free audio at: paulmckenna.com/downloads

1   Imagine a cinema screen in front of you.

2   Next watch a movie on the screen in your
     imagination of a really happy you.

3   Notice your posture, the expression on your
     face and the way you radiate happiness,
     connect with other people and the tone of
     your voice.

4   Next imagine floating into the screen and
     step into your happier self.

5   See through the eyes of your happier self, hear your happy internal dialogue and feel how good it feels to be really happy.

6   Notice where you feel the happiest feeling strongest in your body and imagine giving that feeling a colour.

7   Now spread that colour up through your neck and around your head, down through your chest, arms and legs, to the tips of your toes.

8   Now double the brightness and intensity of the colour and double it again until you are glowing with happiness.

9   Now imagine taking this wonderful feeling of happiness with you into your everyday life, your home life, work life and into the future.

continued

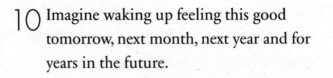

10 Imagine waking up feeling this good tomorrow, next month, next year and for years in the future.

11 Now, while you are in this peak state of mind and body, squeeze your thumb and middle finger together and hold them together while you feel this good. Pause, and take as long as you want, in order to fully experience and remember the amazing feelings that go with it. Do it several times to create a strong associational link.

Congratulations! Now you have connected with your seven super states of self-belief, clarity, determination, connection, creativity, energy & health and happiness and stacked them together to make your ultimate state of being. By now you will be feeling fantastic about your life and if you live in your ultimate state, things will get better and better. As long as you remember to put your thumb and middle finger together to connect with your anchor, you can tap into your ultimate state of being instantly. It will also get stronger and stronger over time. Each time you get yourself into that state of mind, each time you imagine a future from that empowered place, you are creating a new future, a new level of attainment and a new vibration of success throughout your world. So, the more you do it, the better your life will be. So now, take a moment to truly imagine your future through the eyes of your ultimate state. See what now looks possible and the world of opportunity that awaits you. Really take your time to experience how fantastic it feels as you will be living from that dazzling place from this day forward. It's an exciting prospect, isn't it?

The Hypnotic Trance

Now we are at the end of this particular journey, there's just one more thing. If you haven't already, this is the time to listen to the trance.

🔊 Download it for free at:
paulmckenna.com/downloads

Through this powerful induction, I will reinforce all of the positive hypnotic suggestions throughout this book and take your ultimate state of being even deeper so that it becomes an even more essential part of your being. I will also supercharge all of the seven super states that make up your ultimate state of being. Finally, I will boost your energy levels and performance and help enhance your overall wellbeing so you will feel better than you ever thought possible before.

Until we meet…

Paul McKenna

Index of Techniques

Overcoming Self-Sabotage p22 🔊

Step Into Your Role Model p27 🔊

Discovering Your Best Self p33 📝

Experiencing Your True Potential p36 🔊

The Four Zones of Genius p50 📝

Getting In Touch with Your Core Values p58 📝

The Clarity Process p61 📝

Creating A Compelling Future p73 🔊

Discover Your Why **p90** 📝

Aikido One Point Technique **p102**

The Determination Switch **p109** 🔊

Circles Of Connection **p123** 📝

Enhance Your Connections **p134** 🔊

Boost Your Creativity **p147** 🔊

Simple Self-Hypnosis **p167** 🔊

Enhance Your Wellbeing **p169** 🔊

Increase Your Happiness **p190** 🔊

The Hypnotic Trance **p195** 🔊

References

CHAPTER 4

Lieberman, M. D. (2013). *Social: Why our brains are wired to connect.* Crown Publishers/Random House.

CHAPTER 6

Lazarus, N. (2020). *The Lazarus Strategy: How To Age Well and Wisely.* Yellow Kite.

Spiegel, D. et al (1989). Effect of Psychosocial Treatment on Survival of Patients With Metastatic Breast Cancer. *The Lancet.* October, vol 334, issue 8668, pp888–891

Spiegel, D. (2012). Mind matters in cancer survival. *Psycho-Oncology.* June, vol 21, issue 6, pp588–593

Acknowledgements

A book takes an extraordinary amount of time and effort to produce. I would like to thank the following people for their contribution to this project: Sarah Arnold, Mike Osborne, Michael Neill, Neil Reading, Beth Bishop, Caroline Michel, Wayne Davies, Ben Hasler and my wonderful wife Kate McKenna.

Gratitude
Journal

One of the simplest and most powerful things you can do to elevate the base line of your mood is a daily gratitude journal. It can include big things like health, friends and family, or small things like the first cup of tea or coffee in the morning. When you start to consider all the things that you feel grateful for, you are re-enforcing in your mind things that make you feel great. Of course, we get more of what we focus on, so you are training your brain to focus on and search out things that improve your mood. It takes just a few minutes to do each day and then if you are feeling a bit low, just read back through your lists and you will start to feel better.

As with any new habit, you have to push yourself to do it the first few times and then it becomes second nature. That's why the last section of this book contains a 30-day gratitude journal. All you have to do is make a note of 10 things that you feel grateful for – it can be the same or similar every day because the point is to elicit positive feelings connected to your life and re-enforce the good feelings. You remember how we become hardwired through what we continually think about, that's how this approach to journalling works.

Also, it's vitally important for human beings to have a sense of purpose in life. As I mentioned previously, Viktor Frankl famously said, "Purpose is the cornerstone of good mental health." Your purpose is not necessarily your job, although your work is likely to be a part of your purpose. When I was helping people during Covid-19 who had lost their job, I would ask them what their purpose was. For many, it was to be a good spouse, or to be a force for good in the world, or it could just be to strive to be the best version of yourself.

So, also on your gratitude list, it is really important for you to state your purpose. You may have more than one. It may also be your purpose for that day, that week or indeed your life. I cannot emphasise enough how powerful this process is.

Here's an example of my gratitude list for a day.

1. Health, mental/physical.

2. Family.

3. Friends.

4. First cup of tea in the morning.

5. A TV show I am looking forward to watching.

My purpose:

- To be a good husband and friend.

- To be creative.

- To help others.

- To have success in my career.

Now, it's your turn. Set aside a time each day to remember what you are grateful for and make sure to re-read your list regularly.

DAY 1

5 things that I feel grateful for today…

1. _____

2. _____

3. _____

4. _____

5. _____

My purpose tomorrow is:

DAY 2

5 things that I feel grateful for today...

1. _____

2. _____

3. _____

4. _____

5. _____

My purpose tomorrow is:

DAY 3

5 things that I feel grateful for today...

1. _____

2. _____

3. _____

4. _____

5. _____

My purpose tomorrow is:

DAY 4

5 things that I feel grateful for today…

1. _____

2. _____

3. _____

4. _____

5. _____

My purpose tomorrow is:

DAY 5

5 things that I feel grateful for today…

1. _____

2. _____

3. _____

4. _____

5. _____

My purpose tomorrow is:

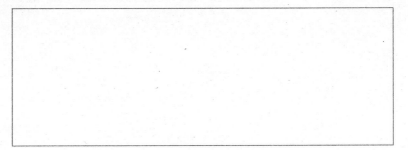

DAY 6

5 things that I feel grateful for today...

1. _____

2. _____

3. _____

4. _____

5. _____

My purpose tomorrow is:

DAY 7

5 things that I feel grateful for today…

1. _____

2. _____

3. _____

4. _____

5. _____

My purpose tomorrow is:

DAY 8

5 things that I feel grateful for today...

1. _____

2. _____

3. _____

4. _____

5. _____

My purpose tomorrow is:

DAY 9

5 things that I feel grateful for today...

1. _____

2. _____

3. _____

4. _____

5. _____

My purpose tomorrow is:

DAY 10

5 things that I feel grateful for today...

1. _____

2. _____

3. _____

4. _____

5. _____

My purpose tomorrow is:

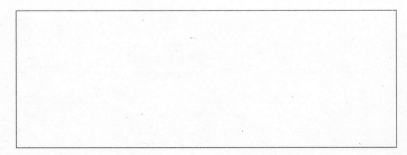

DAY 11

5 things that I feel grateful for today...

1. _____

2. _____

3. _____

4. _____

5. _____

My purpose tomorrow is:

DAY 12

5 things that I feel grateful for today...

1. _____

2. _____

3. _____

4. _____

5. _____

My purpose tomorrow is:

DAY 13

5 things that I feel grateful for today...

1. _____

2. _____

3. _____

4. _____

5. _____

My purpose tomorrow is:

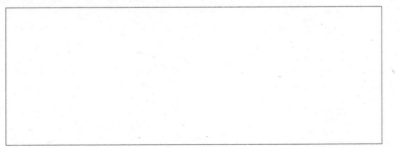

DAY 14

5 things that I feel grateful for today...

1. _____

2. _____

3. _____

4. _____

5. _____

My purpose tomorrow is:

DAY 15

5 things that I feel grateful for today...

1. _____

2. _____

3. _____

4. _____

5. _____

My purpose tomorrow is:

DAY 16

5 things that I feel grateful for today...

1. _____

2. _____

3. _____

4. _____

5. _____

My purpose tomorrow is:

DAY 17

5 things that I feel grateful for today...

1. _____

2. _____

3. _____

4. _____

5. _____

My purpose tomorrow is:

DAY 18

5 things that I feel grateful for today…

1. _____

2. _____

3. _____

4. _____

5. _____

My purpose tomorrow is:

DAY 19

5 things that I feel grateful for today…

1. _____

2. _____

3. _____

4. _____

5. _____

My purpose tomorrow is:

DAY 20

5 things that I feel grateful for today...

1. _____

2. _____

3. _____

4. _____

5. _____

My purpose tomorrow is:

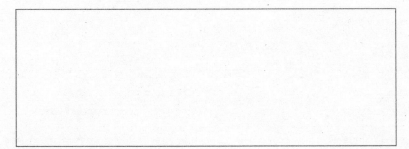

DAY 21

5 things that I feel grateful for today…

1. _____

2. _____

3. _____

4. _____

5. _____

My purpose tomorrow is:

DAY 22

5 things that I feel grateful for today...

1. _____

2. _____

3. _____

4. _____

5. _____

My purpose tomorrow is:

DAY 23

5 things that I feel grateful for today…

1. _____

2. _____

3. _____

4. _____

5. _____

My purpose tomorrow is:

DAY 24

5 things that I feel grateful for today...

1. _____

2. _____

3. _____

4. _____

5. _____

My purpose tomorrow is:

DAY 25

5 things that I feel grateful for today...

1. _____

2. _____

3. _____

4. _____

5. _____

My purpose tomorrow is:

DAY 26

5 things that I feel grateful for today...

1. _____

2. _____

3. _____

4. _____

5. _____

My purpose tomorrow is:

DAY 27

5 things that I feel grateful for today...

1. _____

2. _____

3. _____

4. _____

5. _____

My purpose tomorrow is:

DAY 28

5 things that I feel grateful for today...

1. _____

2. _____

3. _____

4. _____

5. _____

My purpose tomorrow is:

DAY 29

5 things that I feel grateful for today...

1. _____

2. _____

3. _____

4. _____

5. _____

My purpose tomorrow is:

DAY 30

5 things that I feel grateful for today...

1. _____

2. _____

3. _____

4. _____

5. _____

My purpose tomorrow is:

Notes

Notes

Notes

Notes

Notes

Notes